THE Power
OF Parents

Studies in the
Postmodern Theory of Education

Joe L. Kincheloe and Shirley R. Steinberg
General Editors

Vol. 290

PETER LANG
New York • Washington, D.C./Baltimore • Bern
Frankfurt am Main • Berlin • Brussels • Vienna • Oxford

Edward M. Olivos

ᴛʜᴇ **Power**
ᴏꜰ **Parents**

A Critical Perspective
of Bicultural Parent Involvement
in Public Schools

FOREWORD BY ANTONIA DARDER

PETER LANG
New York • Washington, D.C./Baltimore • Bern
Frankfurt am Main • Berlin • Brussels • Vienna • Oxford

Library of Congress Cataloging-in-Publication Data

Olivos, Edward M.
The power of parents: a critical perspective of bicultural parent involvement
in public schools / Edward M. Olivos.
p. cm. — (Counterpoints; v. 290)
Includes bibliographical references and index.
1. Education—Parent participation. 2. Parent-teacher relationships.
3. Home and school. 4. Children of immigrants—Education.
I. Title. II. Series: Counterpoints (New York, N.Y.); v. 290.
LB1048.5.O45   371.103—dc22   2006005797
ISBN 0-8204-7478-9
ISSN 1058-1634

Bibliographic information published by **Die Deutsche Bibliothek**.
Die Deutsche Bibliothek lists this publication in the "Deutsche
Nationalbibliografie"; detailed bibliographic data is available
on the Internet at http://dnb.ddb.de/.

Cover art, La Papaya, by Carmen E. Quintana
Cover design by Lisa Barfield

The paper in this book meets the guidelines for permanence and durability
of the Committee on Production Guidelines for Book Longevity
of the Council of Library Resources.

© 2006 Peter Lang Publishing, Inc., New York
29 Broadway, New York, NY 10006
www.peterlang.com

Printed in the United States of America

Dedicated to: my mother Yolanda, my father José, my brothers José Jr. and Gregory, my girlfriend Victoria, and to the many friends, families, students, and colleagues who have touched my life.

Table of Contents

Foreword

It is impossible to democratize schools without opening them to the real participation of parents and the community in determining the school's destiny.

Paulo Freire[1]

As Paulo Freire reminds us here, the democratization of schools, particularly of those that serve racialized and economically oppressed populations, cannot be achieved without the active participation of parents in shaping the destiny of these schools and communities. Hence, our work with parents must be understood as one of the most significant revolutionary acts that we can carry out as teachers. In carrying out this emancipatory political project, our faith in the capacity of parents as subjects of history is every bit as important as the faith that we extend to their children in the classroom. Without such faith, we risk the danger of objectifying parents and falling prey to the infantilizing parent discourse of public school institutions and the disingenuous manner in which parents are often treated, either by dismissing their concerns or coercing their participation in limiting and often repressive ways.

What is often lost or forgotten even among progressive educators is the incredible power and force that is held in the hands of parents, if they were only to receive the opportunity and support to participate and contribute in meaningful ways. Parent participation is critical to the education of bicultural children and the liberation of culturally and economically subordinated communities from policies and practices that perpetuate their marginalization and exploitation.

Yet, often their parents are instrumentalized and forced into conformity with schooling practices that perpetuate not only their exclusion, but also cultural and linguistic genocide.

In addition, seldom are questions of class privilege and class formation tied to the deep racialization that takes place as a daily lived
experience in communities of color. Gary Orfield's[2] work clearly
testifies to the increasing re-segregation that has been taking place
across the country, despite 40 years of heroic efforts by educators and
community activists to change the segregated nature of public schooling. This is so, because there has been a consistent failure to recognize
school segregation as inextricably linked to the economic apartheid
inherent in the U.S. political economy—namely, capitalism. Hence,
the economic restructuring of the last 20 years and the ferocity of
globalization have left their indelible mark on poor and working class
communities.

Furthermore, the hidden curriculum of assimilation and class inequalities has become even more camouflaged and distorted in much
of the neoconservative buzz on teacher professionalization and school
accountability. Rather than improving the educational conditions
within low-income schools, the ideology of this rhetoric has ultimately served to distance and obstruct the capacity of teachers to
recognize and critically engage with bicultural parents, as both fellow
workers and community members. This separation reinforces hierarchical relations of power within public school districts and the imposition of exclusionary knowledge, worldview, and language practices
on both bicultural children and their parents.

So despite all the hoopla, relationships between teachers as "experts" and bicultural parents have little to do with democratic participation and the building of a mutually respectful ground for
interaction and learning. Instead, traditional views of parent involvement have functioned to perpetuate a sphere of privilege and
control that undermines bicultural parents' self-determination and
the emancipatory role that schools can play in the lives of bicultural
parents and their children. In failing to examine this phenomenon
seriously, educators deny bicultural parents an opportunity to voice
their concerns and to critically interrogate the oppressive conditions
that limit their existence. And beyond this interrogation, it prevents
bicultural parents from any active decision-making within schools
that might potentially shift the locus of control and transform structures of inequality.

By so doing, the culture, language, and affective skills that children and their parents bring to the school, in the interest of their

empowerment as subjects of their learning and their histories, are systematically maligned and eroded. Even more disconcerting is the fact that many discriminatory policies and practices are carried out by well-meaning teachers and administrators. These are agents of schooling who uncritically adopt the rhetoric and practices of "accountability," "high risk" intervention, or "for the good of all children" attitudes that betray their lofty expressions of commitment to diversity, multiculturalism, or social justice.

As a consequence, teacher practice has become more routinized and controlled, while parent input has become more and more structured and monitored. Stringent control of relationships within schools often prevents or hinders teachers' opportunities for meaningful engagement with low-income and working-class bicultural parents. Unfortunately, this can even be the case when teachers come from the very same cultural, class, and linguistic communities as their students, despite being specifically hired for the particular cultural knowledge they bring to the education of Latino, African-American, Asian, Native American or immigrant children. The rewards and punishment system along with the rigid structure of "teaching to the test" curricula is meant to keep teachers in line, with little creative time to develop meaningful, working relationships with parents. To contest this condition requires an insurmountable commitment by teachers to the struggle for democratic life in schools.

Also as unfortunate are the overt and covert deficit notions held by teachers and administrators toward bicultural students; deficit notions extended, by association, to bicultural parents. These misguided notions are propagated, for the most part, devoid of any systematic analysis that directly implicates the oppressive social, economic, political, cultural and linguistic forces that structurally shape and perpetuate the exclusion, exploitation, and domination of bicultural communities. Moreover, deficit notions fail to expose openly the material conditions under which Latino, African-American, Asian, Native American or immigrant populations must struggle daily to contend with the systematic negation of their experiences in schools, by way of tracking, high-stakes testing, and the erasure of their histories, culture, and languages.

Yet, despite the many difficult issues raised by Olivos in *The Power of Parents*, his work reminds us that teachers and administrators must remain ever cognizant that hegemonic domination, as is prevalent within American public schools, is always a partial affair. And since this hegemony of schooling requires the consensus of those most brutally exploited by its antics, issues of social agency, political conscientization, and resistance must be central to teachers' efforts to engage with bicultural parents, in the midst of the political obstacles and hostilities often present within public schools. Moreover, it is through such concerted efforts that a path can be built *with* bicultural parents that nurtures and fortifies conditions for their struggle for empowerment and democratic participation in the educational lives of their children.

It is precisely this struggle to create such a path that is at the heart of *The Power of Parents*. This is a book grounded in Olivos' tireless work with parents and their joint efforts to understand and challenge the impact of assimilative forces in the perpetuation of racism, class inequalities and social exclusion. Moreover, what is quickly evident is that bicultural parents, *together* with teachers, must create a political community to challenge the undemocratic structures of schooling, which more often than not are responsible for the academic failure their children experience in U.S. schools.

The Power of Parents both challenges and interrogates ideas of parent involvement, through contending with the serious conflicts, tensions, and contradictions at work in bicultural parents' efforts to participate more fully in their children's education. Shattering myths that stifle parent involvement in bicultural communities is of utmost concern here. Most importantly, *The Power of Parents* sets out to highlight an essential point—that to ignore the potential impact of parents both to their children's well being and as members of a school community is in direct contradiction to any liberatory educational process. For it is precisely only through those relationships of solidarity established *with* bicultural parents that greater possibilities for school and social transformation can be realized. This is the resounding message, echoed loud and clear, throughout *The Power of Parents*.

Acknowledgments

Writing a book is no easy task, nor is it an individual accomplishment. Many individuals: friends, colleagues, and family members, played a significant role in the completion of this text.

First of all, I need to acknowledge my family who are very important to me: my mother Yolanda, my father José, and my brothers José Jr. and Gregory. They have always been an important part of my personal and professional life.

Besides the members of my family, the person who has had the greatest impact on my work as a teacher and a scholar has been Dr. Alberto M. Ochoa of the Department of Policy Studies in Language and Cross-cultural Education at San Diego State University, my alma mater. His support and encouragement during my career as a public school teacher, a graduate student, and a university professor have helped me reach this incredible goal. I am fortunate to have him as a friend and a mentor. This book would not have been possible without his support.

Also tremendously important to this work have been the following friends and colleagues: Dr. Antonia Darder who challenged my way of thinking and who provided me with much appreciated feedback for this book. Antonia has always unselfishly supported my work as a scholar and an activist and I am indebted to her generosity and inspired by her passion for social justice. Equally important is the support I've received from Dr. Karen Cadiero-Kaplan who held my hand through the publication process of this book. Any time I had a question, Karen was always there to guide me and encourage me. I must also acknowledge Dr. René Núñez who stood alongside me as I worked with parents and community as an elementary school teacher and who showed me how to work in communion with the parents and students I serve.

I also wish to thank my longtime friend Joe Wainio who always stands up for what he feels is right and supports the work of Latino parents in their struggles for educational justice. If it were not for Joe, much of the work I accomplished with parents would not have been possible. The same goes for Tony Garcia, a longtime colleague, friend, and student advocate.

Many thanks to Shirley Steinberg, Joe Kincheloe, Chris Myers, and Bernadette Shade who patiently waited out this text as I struggled during my first year as a tenure track professor at California State University, Dominguez Hills. Thank you for the opportunity to publish my work. I hope the readers enjoy this book as much as I enjoyed writing it.

Thanks and appreciation also need to go out to the parents and students I worked with in San Diego during my career as a public school teacher. Despite obstacles, barriers, and attempts to silence their voices, they have stood tall, proud, and defiant in the face of cultural invasion and exploitation. I have learned a lot from them.

A very special thanks also goes to Dr. Carmen E. Quintana whose beautiful art adorns the cover of this book. *La Papaya* represents survival, nourishment, life, hope, and faith which are elements that daily guide the struggle of living. The papaya is a fruit that nourishes people of color in many third world countries. It represents life and its seeds represent the beads of prayer that in many cultures give people hope, faith, and the search for truth and strength. The symbolism of the lime (of sour flavor) represents the struggle and loneliness that one often confronts in the struggle of survival. The papaya and the lime also represent the tensions and the ongoing challenges that face people, a community or a family, to have the necessary courage and voice to work for social justice and to act as educational warriors (as *guerreros*) in the development of youth. The papaya is a beacon and a reminder that we are all responsible for each other in our struggle to survive and improve the quality of life of our communities.

And finally, but not least, I wish to acknowledge Victoria Sanguino, my girlfriend, who put up with me being locked up in my office for over a year working on this book; who pushed me to finish this work, even when I felt like giving up; and who supports me unquestionably in my professional and personal endeavors, even when it means lonely days and nights for her.

Special acknowledgement: The figure "Defining the Concept of Resistance," comes from Solórzano, D. & Delgado Bernal, D, *Urban Education*, Vol. 36 No. 3, May 2001, 308-342 © Corwin Press, Inc. Reprinted by Permission of Corwin Press Inc.

A Case Study of Bicultural Parent Involvement

My work with parents seeks to understand the tensions that lead to conflicts between bicultural parents and their children's schools and why these parents at times resist the efforts of the school personnel. Significant in my area of work with parents is the self-organization of bicultural parents into autonomous parent organizations which struggle to hold their children's schools more accountable. The groups that I have worked with usually work outside of the school system in that they hold their meetings and do their advocacy off the school grounds and without the "consent" or influence of the site administrator or district personnel.

In my 2003 study[1] I document how a small group of Latino parents form a parent organization independent of their children's school. I detail how after repeated attempts to dialogue with the school administration on meaningful topics and to have a say in the decision-making process at their site, these particular parents started having their own education meetings off campus. At these meetings the parents would openly discuss concerns they had with the school, and certain members of the staff, and strategize how they could go about rectifying them.

These parents' hard work, persistence, and political understanding of the problems at hand led them to become action researchers and education advocates. My particular fascination with this group was that they became significantly powerful and well connected in their district, despite being small in numbers, to the point that they were able to effectively hold their children's school accountable for a quality education and move forward their agenda. Moreover, the principal at their site was eventually replaced upon the parents' continuous urging. This group even went on to publish a monthly newsletter on the critical situation of Latino students in their school district which garnered the attention of many high level district administrators, including the superintendent.

Below is a brief recollection of my experiences with these individuals to demonstrate how they worked to transform their situation and the situation at their children's school.

A Teacher's Reflection

Teachers such as myself who have worked any significant amount of time in low-income, bicultural communities have witnessed first-hand the inequities and inequalities which are found in the public school system: student academic underachievement, lack of appropriate teaching materials, low teacher expectations, high turnover of staff and students, unattractive physical conditions of the school sites, school violence, etc.[2] These injustices are evident, and many bicultural parents recognize them.

Mrs. Cervantes,[3] one of the parents from the San Diego parent group I worked with, stated that bicultural parents "begin to notice the difference [in their children's schools] right away. 'We don't have this. They[4] do. This we don't have either, but they do.' One notices that the differences begin all the way from the streets."

Despite the fact that the injustices in the public school system appear to be so obvious, and I have heard many bicultural parents express similar sentiments throughout the years, why is it that only a small number of bicultural parents openly question the U.S. public school system—a system which has historically failed their children in disproportionate numbers? And why does it seem that even fewer bicultural parents openly challenge it?

My initial experiences of working with bicultural parents began in 1993 when I began work as a bilingual education teacher in an inner-city school in San Diego, and where my early efforts to involve the Latino parents in school-related activities often failed due to low attendance and/or low participation. My initial assumptions, which I would use to explicate this phenomenon, were founded on deficit thinking.[5] I somehow believed that Latino parents didn't come to the school because they did not value or have an interest in their children's education; that they weren't educated enough to understand their important role in the education of their children; or that they were just ungrateful for the extra hours I was putting forth to hold extracurricular meetings and workshops for them.

I soon learned, however, through my personal experiences with this small group of low-income Latino parents and my school district's resistance to their active participation that my initial assumptions were wrong. These parents did indeed have an interest and desire to participate in their children's education; what they lacked, as did I, was the political consciousness necessary to grasp how the school system implicitly (and explicitly) works to discourage the active, authentic, and meaningful involvement of low-income, bicultural parents and their communities. It was during this time that I began my work to try to understand what exactly is implied in current perceptions of parent involvement and how it differs markedly depending on the social and cultural context of the community.

A Teacher's Role

I began my work as the faculty advisor of the English Learner Advisory Committee (ELAC) at my school with the principal's consent during the 1998–1999 school year. During this time certain incidents were occurring at the school site that had many Latino parents feeling alienated and unwanted—this at a school which at the time was over 80% Latino. At these meetings a particularly vocal group of parents, comprised of six parents, would often express to me their concerns. They would complain that the office staff mistreated and disrespected the Spanish-speaking Latino parents; that the principal lacked the cultural and linguistic understanding of the community and as a result many of the Latino parents felt alienated, thus unwilling to participate at the school; and that the administrators, both at the site as well as the district level, completely excluded the Latino parent majority from any significant decisions that affected *their* school.

Given the concerns that were being raised at the ELAC meetings by this group of parents, as well as at other school-sponsored parent meetings, I saw the opportunity to challenge the popular assumption that Latino parents do not want to participate in the education of their children. Indeed, it appeared to me that I had come across a group of Latino parents who were clearly willing, eager, and "capable" of participating in school related matters. Moreover, the principal and my fellow teachers would often share at staff meetings their desire to have parents more involved at the school. Thus, this was the perfect opportunity for me to make both sides happy.

My work as the ELAC advisor began by creating an environment at the monthly meetings in which the parents were free to express their concerns without the fear of being criticized, slighted, or ignored. At these meetings, I would pose questions to the parents as to why they felt these events were happening and what they believed could, and should, be done to rectify the problems. And while I definitely made it clear to the parents throughout this process that I felt the school belonged to the community and that they had the right and the power to make the changes they felt were in the best interest of their children, I purposely held back from specifically telling the parents what to do. Reflecting back, I feel that this was the right thing to do. To be sure, it has become my experience that when Latino parents show public dissatisfaction about school policies or assert their rights a common assumption among school personnel is that there is someone "behind them" serving as an outside agitator, "using them" for their benefit.

There was a lot of suspicion in my work with Latino parents among both staff and parents. This feeling of suspicion about teachers and their alliances with parents was evident from Latino parents who in the beginning were distrustful of why a teacher or staff member would be willing to "help" them, as demonstrated in the following words which were expressed by Mrs. Medina:

> With all due respect for the teachers who are here, I sometimes think that teachers, who I understand have a very difficult job, are here at the meeting out of convenience. Not all, but many, are probably here because they have a problem at their school or with their principal and they want the parents to support them or to help them get out of a jam. I've seen this at other meetings [like this one], the teachers only show up when there is some sort of problem.

Understanding the lack of trust that often exists, and is created, between teachers and parents my initial work with these parents consisted of listening to their concerns and supporting their efforts to resolve them. Oftentimes I would even work as an intermediary between the parents and the administration since I held the belief that both shared the same agenda: to have the children at the school succeed academically. During the first few months of 1999, as more and more Latino parents began to directly raise their particular issues, resistance and suspicion on the part of the school administration also became apparent.

This resistance against the parents becoming more critically involved at the school took on many forms. At first the site administrators would frequently just ignore the parents' concerns, hoping that they would somehow tire and go away. Other times, the administrators would try to convince the parents that their complaints were misguided—there were no problems at the school, or the problems they spoke of were individual cases and not school-wide phenomena. In the rare instances in which the administrators would actually acknowledge the parents' concerns, the principal and the vice-principal would provide them with false promises of an "investigation." In reality, the only investigation the administration ever conducted was among the staff to see who was "talking to the parents." It was a process, a long process, the administrators would often tell the parents.

The site and district-level administrators' responses to the parents' concerns helped raise their political consciousness as they began to question the sincerity of the administrators, as well as the district's public assertion about valuing parent involvement. In other words, when they began to experience a personal experience dissonance between their lived experiences and what the school promoted as meaningful parent involvement, they began to realize the insincerity of the school's parent involvement policies and practices. It was through these lived experiences with the contradictions found in the school's messages and policies for involving parents that they witnessed firsthand how bicultural parents are treated in the schools. Several of the parents even began to identify and name the tactics used by administrators to detract them from their advocacy.

Every administrator has the same tactics to distract us. We had the opportunity to have several meetings with the district superintendent and it was the same thing. He would show up, say what he had to say, and leave. Every time we would have our meetings with him, we'd get worried because we knew that we would not have the time to ask our questions or have them answered. He would do all the talking. All administrators use this tactic.

As these events were taking place at the school, many of my initial assumptions about Latino parents began to change. I had previously assumed that the reason for the lack of parent involvement at my school exclusively lay in the parents' desire and/or commitment to participate, never before had I thought about questioning the school personnel's treatment of these parents or the sincerity of the school's policies and practices which claimed to value meaningful parent involvement. Soon thereafter I began to believe that there was something deeper to the relationship between Latino parents and the public schools, something that required a more global view of this relationship.

Steps toward Empowerment and Transformation

Initially, this group of Latino parents worked in "secret," only sharing their concerns with parents who were their friends or with sympathetic teachers such as myself. It wasn't until the late winter of 1999 that this group of Latino parents actually began to directly raise their concerns to the school administration. Feeling that the school was excluding them, the parents decided to directly express their concerns in writing—itself a rare occurrence among Latino parents. This was a powerful statement on the part of the parents as they began to realize the importance of the written word and the practices of the dominant culture, as expressed in the words of Mrs. González:

> Everything we accomplished, we were able to do under certain rules. We have been learning a lot. We've learned to document everything in writing and to sign it. The wind will blow away our words, so everything we have to say to the administrators we also write. Our children have the right to have it all, that's why we are no longer mothers; we are now investigators in child development and human relations!

The first set of concerns the parents expressed in writing to the school administrator were done with the help of another school employee sympathetic to the parents' struggles. This first letter dealt with school aesthetics and non-instructional issues such as the cleanliness of the bathrooms, the physical environment of the school grounds, and the treatment of their children in the cafeteria. Responses to inquiries of this nature would seem to be normal and superficial in nature. That is, one would imagine that such issues would be non-threatening to the school administration, particularly since these issues do not question the power of the principal or the organizational structure of the administration. Yet, responses given to this group's concerns proved, according to the parents, inappropriate or insincere. Specifically, the principal met with the group of parents several weeks later during a Parent Coffee[6] meeting to "discuss" their concerns. Her response, according to the parents, was an acknowledgment of the issues of concern where she elaborated that these issues, while important, would be investigated but that nothing could be promised in light of other more pressing academic concerns.

After several weeks and still no remedy to the issues of concern or follow-through by the administration to the initial letter/petition, the parent group began to question the sincerity of the principal and her desire to work with the Latino community. Also at this time one parent leader in particular began to notice serious academic violations. In fact, during this time most of these parents' eyes were beginning to open on to other issues at the school. In a sense, these parents were beginning to develop a critical perspective when it came to the functioning of the school and the opportunities being afforded to their children and they began to purposefully seek out issues at the school that needed to be rectified.

In one incident, during the late winter/early spring of 1999, one of the mothers in the group noticed that her daughter, who had an IEP (Individualized Educational Program) was being left without special education services when the special education teacher would go "off track" for three weeks with no attempt being made by the principal to find a substitute, nor was there any communication to the parents whose children were being affected about this issue. Such negligence by the principal led this mother to comment that if this "were any other school" this type of thing wouldn't be happening.

The following week, with the help of another parent, the mother brought this issue up at a Parent Coffee. The response given to her at this meeting was that this was an individual concern and that it should be discussed privately. No other parents needed to know about this. She was advised to set up an appointment with the principal. It became apparent to this mother at this moment that an effort was being made to prevent her emerging consciousness from spreading. Moreover, she expressed that she was being denied a voice in her child's education.

After several months of continued dialogue and growing tension between the school and the parent leaders, the parent group finally scored a victory. Given this mother's persistence with the special education issue, all special education staff would begin working twelve-month calendars, and special education students would not be left without services during the teacher's absence. As a response to this negligence, the parents also filed an official complaint with the United States Office of Civil Rights claiming lack of due process, differential treatment for Latino parents, and academic violations. This complaint was very instrumental in strengthening the voices of the parents. It showed the district that what this parent group lacked in financial and political strength they made up for in resilience and persistence. Indeed, it caused the district to take notice.

These activities of letter writing, making an official complaint, and direct communication with the school administrators were important steps toward empowerment for many of these parents. In fact, as a result of their work many of these parents began to understand how the school system explicitly and implicitly functions to detract them from their work as political and educational advocates. I vividly recall how proud these parents were with this victory, particularly when they realized that they possessed the desire and the skills to change the direction of their children's school and contribute positively to their success. These were important steps toward empowerment for these parents in that they began to see themselves as powerful and knowledgeable individuals and wholly as an empowered group.

Organizing for Empowerment

The leaders of this parent group formed a tight-knit group. It consisted of four mothers, one father, and one grandmother. All were Latinos (Mexicans) and all, but one (the grandmother), were immigrants to this country. On the issue of language, two of the parents felt fairly comfortable with English and one was fluent in both languages (the grandmother). Also, many of the parent leaders of this group occupied school leadership positions such as membership on the ELAC, School Site Council (SSC), and the School Governance Team (SGT).

During the summer of 1999 these parents also became an "official" group. They were meeting frequently at a nearby church discussing strategies to have their voices heard. At these meetings, the parent leaders would share their concerns with other parents who were not keeping up with what was going on at the school. Moreover, they were building support among the community leaders and with more of the teachers at the site. In fact, a local priest as well as a local restaurant owner openly supported these parents' efforts with letters to the principal and to the school board.

During this time the parents also established communication with a Mexican American educational advocacy group that consisted of university professors and community advocates. Their goal was to share with this group the concerns they had at the school as well as to gain political support for their efforts. Not surprisingly, this advocacy group became one of the parents' strongest supporters and was instrumental in arranging important meetings with influential organizations and individuals within the district as well as the city of San Diego.

This Latino parent group became a powerful group in their school and school district. Throughout the remainder of the year, and during the following years, they had continuous meetings with the principal, district personnel, school board members, and the district superintendent to discuss issues of concern. Their concerns even began to encompass district-wide issues related to the disproportionate retention rate of students of color, bilingual education, and academic rigor at low-performing schools.

Yet, how did this power materialize? How did a small group of Latino parents who just one year prior had accepted the dictates of the school without opposition get to a level of critical and transformational consciousness? And, how did they manage to stay on course and dedicated to their original mission of improving their children's schools?

Obviously, a motivating force for the parents was the treatment they had been receiving from the school and the district as they tried to authentically participate in the education of their children. For in spite of their legitimate complaints and concerns about the school, efforts to remedy them were non-existent. In fact, a common response to their complaints was a common one—nothing. In other words, they were ignored in the hope that they would eventually tire out and go away. One of the parent leaders described her experiences of dealing with the school as "going around in circles" in that they never got a concrete response from the school or the school district to any of their concerns.

It is therefore important to acknowledge these types of experiences in which a subordinate individual or group is able to name the contradictions within their social environment and choose a path of resistance that will transform the situation that the true empowerment process begins.

Empowerment Is in the Eye of the Beholder

The educational work that documents the empowerment process of bicultural parents acknowledges the importance of their ability to effectively intervene academically and socially on their children's behalf. In my opinion, however, this position greatly limits the potential the word empowerment has. Parent empowerment should not only been seen as a process that allows marginalized parents to better support, without question, the agenda of the school. Instead, it should be the growth of political strength that allows them to take up their own struggle when they feel they are being overlooked or wronged. However, unfortunately there is still little research literature out there that documents the political empowerment process of bicultural parents when they decide to challenge their school or their school district. Moreover, there is even less that addresses the issue of how bicultural parents can empower themselves given their lack of financial and political resources. Therefore, while the term empowerment has been used in recent literature to describe the birth of a social consciousness within an individual or group, few have been able to document this process and this is a sorely needed area for parent advocates and their supporters.

What made this group of Latino parents an important advocacy group was their persistence and resilience. Having built a history of action and advocacy this little group began to grow until it reached district-wide proportion. "This community is ours," said Mrs. Cervantes, one of the parent leaders of this group, when asked why she didn't give up despite the barriers they initially encountered. Her work and her dealings with the school district developed in her a deep sense of advocacy for her community. This, however, was not without frustration and setbacks. Also, this empowerment process did not occur because the school and the school district decided to share power but rather because the parents decided to use theirs in an effort to reclaim their voice and their children's future.

"We are going to continue in this community and our children are going to grow up here." Hence, as a community leader, Mrs. Cervantes realized that the school is not a separate entity of the community that belongs to a far away district but instead is an integral part of it. The thought of the school belonging to the community instead of the school district is difficult for many educators to understand. Indeed, many that work in the field of education unfortunately still fail to question the oppressive premise that views the school as the savior of bicultural communities. Instead they unwillingly often buy into, support, and participate in oppressive practices. The implications of dealing authentically and sincerely with bicultural communities entail entering into a process of authentic dialogue with them.

Within this book I will argue that the process of authentic dialogue between bicultural parents and the schools will *not* occur without tension or conflict. School leaders and policymakers can decide the path this tension will take, however: toward the collaborative empowerment of all those involved, particularly the students, or the disintegration of the schools' purpose and reputation in their respective communities. The answer to this dilemma will not be made from the top-down or without the integration of the bicultural communities in question as we shall see in the following chapters.

Finally, this book is written in eight chapters. Each of following seven chapters provides a "piece of the pie" to understanding why bicultural parents often do not participate in high numbers in their children's schools and why school personnel tend to resist them when they do. At the end of each chapter questions for reflection or critical incidents are provided to help the reader interact with the issues presented.

It is expected that while the frameworks provided within this book will help the educator theoretically understand the complex relationship between bicultural parents and the public schools, the actual context in which the phenomenon is taking place will provide the critical elements for developing a parent involvement orientation that will challenge previous oppressive and shortsighted techniques which up to now have done nothing to improve the quality of education for bicultural students in our nation.

Questions for Reflection
1. How do you define parent involvement?
2. What does parent involvement "look like?"
3. What are the benefits of parent involvement?
4. What role should teachers assume in their involvement with parents?
5. Should the teachers' role be limited so as not to "overly influence" the parents?

Bicultural Parents in the Public Schools

This book is about parents, specifically, "bicultural" parents, and their relationship with the public school system as well as *my* work with them. In this book you will also "hear" the voices of bicultural parents whom I have worked with as they explain in their own words what they have experienced as they have tried to work authentically and collaboratively with their children's schools in an effort to effect change. I have collected these voices and stories, and have developed the theories you will read in this book, over the past ten years as I've worked alongside bicultural parents in their struggle for educational justice for their children.

My work with parents comes from my experiences as a student, an elementary school teacher, and a university professor.[1] This book is therefore part reflection, part theory, part narrative, and part political activism. One caveat to the reader, however, before we delve completely into the topic at hand. The reader of this text must be aware that while this book is about parent involvement, its main purpose is not to propose a list of approaches, remedies, suggestions, or "promising practices" for engaging historically underrepresented parents. Rather, the purpose of this book is to encourage and challenge you, the reader, to think about your preconceived notions about what parent involvement is and what it constitutes, as well as to encourage you to reflect on your relationship with your students' parents, particularly any biases you may have.

I chose this path for this book because for me the term "parent involvement" has far too often been diluted in the professional literature and in practice to a laundry list of activities that the "experts" feel good parents "do" to blindly support the schools' agendas. It is not my intent to repeat this practice. Rather my purpose here is to provide a framework with which the reader can critically analyze the relationship between the public schools and bicultural parents, as well as lay out a potential framework for developing a more "transformational" relationship between the two. This concept will be explained in greater detail in the chapters to follow. But before we turn our attention to the pending matter, a few definitions need to be clarified.

Book Terminology

Many terms have been used to describe low-income students, students of color, and their communities. The most common ones in the professional literature and in social policy are *minority, underprivileged, at risk,* and *disadvantaged.* From a more critical perspective, the terms *subordinate, oppressed,* and *bicultural* have also been used. All of these terms carry with them clear political and ideological connotations. Thus, for my purposes, unless I am quoting a source directly, you will notice that I prefer to use the latter terms (or other similar ones) to refer to our ethnically diverse parent and student populations. I do this because the former terms "linguistically, and hence politically, [reflect and perpetuate] a view of subordinate cultures as deficient and disempowered."[2] It is not my intent to do this; rather my goal here is to shed a critical light on what has often been construed in the professional literature as "the problem of minority parent involvement."

The term bicultural will be used to refer to, in general, individuals or social groups who live and "function in two [or more] distinct sociocultural environments: their primary culture, and that of the dominant mainstream culture of the society in which they live."[3] Moreover, in those instances in which I want to emphasize the issues of class and asymmetrical power relations, I prefer to use the term "subordinate" or "oppressed." Whatever the term, however, let it be understood that this book is about any member of society who has systemically and historically been placed at a disadvantage by virtue of their class, race, ethnicity, gender, immigrant status, or sexual orientation. It is to those communities which have been disempowered to authentically participate in the education of their children and have suffered the consequences that this book is dedicated.

The Challenges of Public Education

Public education is an interesting institution. Many criticize it as failing and as a burden on public taxpayers, while others scrutinize it for being unfair and inequitable to certain social groups, and still others advocate for it as a necessary institution for the functioning of a free and democratic society. So, who is correct? Is public education really failing and is it really in a crisis? Is our public education system failing to produce the people with the talent and the skills that are needed to maintain our position of dominance in the world? Or is the public education system in the United States actually working, serving its function?

Indeed, nobody can argue with the fact that today our country is still the strongest and most powerful nation in the world. We are the richest nation in the world as demonstrated by our capital influence in the consumption, exportation and importation of material goods and resources. We are also a culturally powerful nation as demonstrated by the hegemonic force of our movies, music, and language over many parts of the world. And finally, we are a militarily powerful nation as demonstrated by our ability to invade other countries with impunity.

Certainly, I would not be wrong in my assumption if I were to claim that many of the people who made our country so powerful are most likely products of the public school system. So, now I ask: what appears to be the problem? Well, perhaps the problem is that there are several myths driving our public school system, myths that perpetuate a constant and consistent underachievement of certain social groups. This inconsistency in achievement between the dominant white population and bicultural groups has often been referred to as the "achievement gap." This achievement gap is an important area of study in that it demonstrates a pattern of generational academic and social underachievement, yet all too often the achievement gap has been studied superficially, with a focus on the obvious rather than on the structural.

The achievement gap has been the topic of much debate for many years and has resulted in quite a number of theories and discussions which have attempted to explain why students of color fail to achieve academically, socially, and economically in such large numbers. All this talk among politicians and policymakers has led to a series of interventions and reforms throughout the past five decades which have often either centered on the academic programs of the schools or the influence of bicultural parents and communities in the school context, or both. To date, however, none of these efforts have served to adequately reverse the trend of bicultural student school failure.

The cause of the achievement gap between bicultural, low-income students and middle- and upper-class whites has long been debated between two distinct camps, one liberal and one conservative.[4] In a general sense, conservative educational reforms have for the most part been focused on individual and group characteristics. This focus on characteristics such as initiative, merit, intelligence, talent, and personal accountability proposes that failure is often an individual or group choice. Those who fail within the current system of education have only themselves to blame for not being able to take advantage of it, and the solution is that they must put forth more effort and dedication if they are to reap the rewards. In short, conservative policymakers generally believe that those who fail to succeed academically and socially must be held more accountable for their actions and personal choices. Accordingly, conservative education reforms often consist of implementing more high-stakes testing and higher "expectations" so that individuals are held more accountable for their learning.

Liberals, on the other hand, recognize that there are different positions of privilege within society and argue that the subordinate groups are "lacking" what the dominant group possesses. In their view, subordinate groups merely need a "step up" in order to access mainstream institutions. Thus liberal solutions for the academic achievement gap tend to propose compensatory programs that will help "disadvantaged" groups acquire the dominant cultural capital. In other words, liberals propose that efforts must be made to "change the victim." This liberal stance, however, fails to acknowledge the inherent injustices found in the current technocratic/capitalist system, arguing instead for programs that will help subordinate groups overcome their "disadvantaged" status.

In opposition to these two camps this book proposes that bicultural student underachievement and low bicultural parent participation are the result of a complex socioeconomic and historic *structure of dominance*.[5] That is, I contend that the U.S. education system is part of complex system of domination which creates and recreates asymmetrical power relations based on race, class, and gender, and that the most effective way to "combat" this system is to become cognizant of the contradictions found within it. Therefore, in this book I argue that bicultural parents must begin to understand their roles within the socioeconomic and historic context from which their subordination and their children's academic failure arises if they are to effectively contribute to the transformation of the school system. Moreover, bicultural parents need to participate in the schools in a manner that will challenge the school system to meet the needs of all students while also effecting social change and tension. Stated simply, the academic achievement gap will not close unless those parents whose children have historically failed within this system make explicit efforts to change the manner in which their children are being educated and socialized into the menial labor jobs of society.

Issues in Parent Involvement

While the term and current perception of parent involvement may be fairly new to the modern school context, families have long been an integral component in the academic and social success of their children. In the United States there exists a long history of parents actively participating in the education of their children, with parent educational organizations being established at the national level as far back as the late 1880s. Yet, given this long history of parents being involved in their children's education, why is it that the public school system has consistently been unsuccessful in establishing an authentic relationship with the communities it serves, particularly "hard to reach" parents, i.e., African-Americans, Latinos, immigrants, and low-income parents? And why is it that educators who work in urban and bicultural school settings still find themselves asking questions like: Why aren't these parents more involved? Or, why don't these parents care? And conversely, why do parents who *do* participate, particularly bicultural parents, often feel that their participation is meaningless or disingenuous? In fact, we should pose the question directly: why should parents even be involved at their children's schools in the first place? Shouldn't they just leave the education of children up to the experts?

Well, part of the answer to these questions is that nowadays educational literature abounds with professional studies that promote the importance of parent involvement in the education of children. Many in the field of education and public policy are convinced that involving parents in their children's formal education is one of the most beneficial interventions for their academic success.[6] In fact, among the many solutions proposed for improving the quality of public education, parental involvement appears high on many lists for reversing past trends of bicultural student academic underachievement.

Notwithstanding the body of research supporting parent/community involvement, parent involvement in the public school system has long been characterized by certain issues that make specific assumptions about its general effectiveness problematic, particularly when referencing bicultural parents and communities. One of these "issues" is related to the "appropriate roles of family and community members in connections with the schools."[7] Specifically, educators and policymakers often find themselves debating: What rights do parents legally and morally have in regard to how the school system functions? Should parents be allowed to have an equal voice and power status at the schools in par with the "experts?" Furthermore, how far reaching should the influence of parents be in how the schools choose to educate children and whose responsibility should it be when educational attainment is unsuccessful?

These types of questions have led to a functional as well as a conceptual gap in thinking and practice when it comes to parent involvement, particularly since it often appears that both parents and school personnel have a fundamentally different and sometimes contradictory view of what parent involvement is or what it entails. This brings us to the second issue, which is the emphasis placed on school-centered definitions of family and community involvement.

Family and community involvement for many educators often means working to "reach goals defined by the schools (administrators and teachers) that reflect only school values and priorities."[8] This practice is problematic, however, since districts and schools have long identified a narrow band of acceptable behaviors and attitudes that will be tolerated as "legitimate" forms of parental involvement. The kind of involvement school personnel are looking for is participation which is "supportive of school policies and instructional practices"[9] and non-critical. In the public school setting it is clearly understood that if parents are to be involved in school-related matters, than they should always support, not question; follow, not lead; and trust, not doubt. Indeed, if "parents express ideas, values, and norms that are contrary to the dominant view, then their behavior will be regarded with concern."[10]

For example, a parent who helps their child at home with homework is considered an "involved parent," a parent who attends school sponsored events is a considered an "involved parent," a parent who volunteers in their child's classroom is considered an "involved parent." Yet, a parent who is critical of the school and of the underlying detrimental school climate is considered an "obtrusive parent" or worse yet a "troublemaker."

Parent involvement is also often characterized quantitatively rather than qualitatively. That is, administrators and school personnel are often more satisfied with the number of parents in attendance at Open House, on fieldtrips as volunteers, and at assemblies rather than on the quality of the parents' participation in more meaningful roles such as decision-making and advising as part of school governance committees.

And finally, the outcomes of "effective" parental involvement are frequently centered on individual student academic achievement, as in parents helping their *own* children succeed academically. And while individual student academic achievement should indeed be an important goal of parent participation at the schools, I believe that so too is helping parents, particularly ethnically diverse parents, understand and promote their personal process of empowerment and efficacy as well as their children's educational rights. This idea of parents as student advocates and political activists is not entirely new, I understand, yet it does require us to break the longstanding traditional molds and mindsets of what we believe parents, especially low-income, ethnically diverse parents are capable of understanding or entitled to do.

The Need for Bicultural Parent Involvement

A significant layer of complexity is added to the aforementioned issues when the families in question come from bicultural backgrounds.[11] This, of course, is of particular importance in our contemporary public school setting where a high ratio of ethnic, racial, linguistic, economic, and religious diversity is found, and where "failing schools" have brought on the urgency of school reform and accountability. Indeed, no one can deny that the public education system in our country is becoming increasingly diverse. One look into the classrooms of the public schools and you get a glimpse at the future face of America. Students and communities that were once considered the "minority" are in fact becoming, or already are, the "majority" in many urban cities and school districts. Recent data from by the U.S. Department of Education reports, for example, that 69 percent of students in the 100 largest school districts in the United States are bicultural, i.e., nonwhite.[12]

A crucial area of attention for educators should therefore be the dynamic nature of how bicultural parent populations relate to the public school system in general and their children's schools in particular. By the same token attention must also be paid to how school personnel relate to them. In other words, educators must not only attempt to understand more clearly how bicultural parents perceive their roles in the education of their children but also how school personnel treat and interact with family members who are non-middle- or upper-class and nonwhite. This reflection process means that school personnel need to critique and significantly alter traditional practices found in current day parent/school relationships.

In order to develop this deeper clarity concerning the roles of bicultural parents in the education of their children, two distinct arenas of parent involvement must be explored.[13] The first of these arenas is the direct effect that bicultural parents have on their children as their primary source of nurture and socialization; the second concerns their role in the production of education at the school. In regard to the former, a significant body of research has acknowledged that the home of the bicultural child is a rich social and cultural context of learning and cognition, even if it differs from that of the dominant culture.[14] Moreover, it has been argued that even in the poorest of homes, school-like literacy and learning activities are present as well as "alternative conceptualizations of involvement activity" which are often not recognized by the schools.[15]

In addition to the social, moral and academic support bicultural families provide their children in the home, the second arena of involvement for bicultural parents implies that it is similarly important to understand the role bicultural parents can play in improving the quality and effectiveness of education at the school site by making it more responsive to their and their children's needs. Indeed,

> several studies [have] found that families of all income and education levels, and from all ethnic and cultural groups, are engaged in

supporting their children's learning at home. White, middle-class families, however, tend to be more involved at school. [Thus], supporting more involvement at school from all parents may be an important strategy for addressing the achievement gap.[16]

Thus, there appears to be a desperate need to have underrepresented parents become more vigilant and active participants in school-related matters such as school policy, decision-making, and accountability, particularly if failing schools are to be transformed to meet the needs of all students and communities.[17] This need, however, while easily identifiable is not so easily attained and throughout this book we will study those factors which I believe must be addressed if bicultural parents are to become active participants in the education system.

A Conceptual Framework for Bicultural Parent Involvement

One of the goals of this book is to propose critical ways to look at bicultural parent involvement in the schools and at the origins as to why these parents may not appear to be as involved at the schools as we would like. In addition, it also argues that there is an urgent need to have bicultural parents actively and politically involved in their children's schools, surpassing commonly accepted present-day low-impact levels of participation.

The central focus of this book is the *Paradigm of Tension, Contradiction, and Resistance* (Figure 1) that I developed over the last few years. I originally proposed this framework to theorize about, and help elucidate, the "root causes" of low levels of Latino parent involvement in the public school system.[18] It was offered to help explain the relationship between Latino parents and the school system using a structural perspective, and to contradict the assumptions posed by many in the field of education who view the "absence" of Latino parents in the schools as disinterest or incompetence.

I believe that this paradigm, or framework, can also help contextualize the relationship all bicultural parents have with the school system for it takes into account social, economic, and historical influences, thus expanding the analysis to involve diverse issues of class and ethnic relations This paradigm is therefore a map that helps illustrate how the relationship between bicultural parents and the school system is in fact a "micro-reflection" of deeper societal contradictions resulting from economic exploitation and racism. I argue that these contradictions produce ever-present tensions, which eventually develop into conflicts, which are demonstrated either through resistance or active oppositional behavior, when the contradictions become so apparent that they can no longer be ignored or when the subordinate groups "uncover" them as the result of developing a critical and political consciousness.

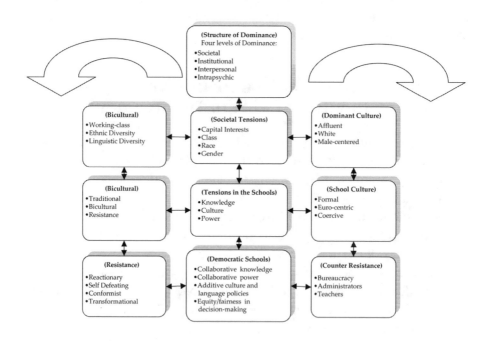

Figure 1: Paradigm of Tension, Contradiction and Resistance in Parent Involvement

Questions for Reflection

1. What should be the ultimate goal of parent involvement?
2. What are some of the challenges of involving bicultural parents in the public schools?

3. Why would bicultural parents not participate in the public schools in large numbers?
4. What can the school personnel do to promote "effective" bicultural parent participation?

A Structural Analysis

I make a fairly simple claim in this book, and that is that the subordinate roles bicultural parents occupy within the school system are a reflection of the subordinate roles they occupy in broader society, and in order to understand the relationship between the two one must take a broader look at the issue. This approach means that we must disregard the artificial barriers that separate schools from society and the optimistic and naïve beliefs that the "disempowered" in our society will somehow authentically be admitted into the school system, or any other state-sponsored institution, as "empowered" equals.

A guiding assumption found within this book is that the relationship between bicultural parents and the public school system is reflective of a larger societal framework of tension, contradictions, and resistance. And for that reason, finding a "solution" for how to involve more low-income bicultural parents in the public schools to improve the academic performance and social achievement of their children must be grounded not only in school interventions but in social and political activism as well. Stated briefly, the effective participation of low-income bicultural parents in school-related matters will ultimately be tied to their effective participation in social and civic society.[1]

It's been my experience that lacking within most pieces of educational literature which speak to the issue of parent involvement in general and bicultural parent involvement in particular is a deeper analysis of the socioeconomic and historical context under which this phenomenon is taking place. Indeed, de-contextualizing school problems has long been common practice in educational literature and public policy, and this has created a very fragmented picture when seeking solutions, as demonstrated by the words of Feinberg and Soltis:

> Whatever the particular controversy in education may be, it is often the case that insufficient attention is paid to the social context in which the issues take on importance. There is a strong tendency to overlook social, political, and cultural factors that have helped create

the situation—and that also serve to create both possibilities for and limitations on what schools and teachers can do at any particular time.[2]

For this reason, a comprehensive analysis of the relationship between bicultural parents and the United States' public school system cannot be limited to the classroom, the school campus, or even the school community. Rather, in order to authentically study this relationship a structural and historical analysis is needed; one which positions these parents as well as the entire school community (i.e., teachers, students, administrators, superintendents, board members, etc.) as agents found within a complex social system.

Given this line of reasoning, in this chapter I will lay out a structural and integrated theoretical foundation which addresses bicultural parent involvement within a social and institutional context. This theory will serve to challenge the beliefs of many in public education and public policy that view the "absence" of bicultural parents in the school system as a sign of apathy or ineptitude. Moreover, it will put into context why past and current literature promoting "promising practices" or "national standards" is insufficient if bicultural parents are to truly change the nature of education in our country.

A Structural Analysis

There is a contention by certain educators and educational theorists alike that the public education system is an instrument of society.[3] These theorists argue in a general sense that schools serve to enhance and maintain the political, social, and ideological elements needed to maintain a stratified economic and political society. Stated differently, these scholars believe that "the process of schooling is a form of 'social and cultural reproduction' that is linked openly to other structures in society, especially economic structures, which reproduce social relations."[4]

If we choose to analyze the public education system through this socioeconomic structural lens, this means that we must take into consideration certain specific fundamental assumptions regarding the role of individuals and institutions as determined by socioeconomic conditions, particularly capitalism. For within capitalist systems, economic conditions are seen as central to human activity at many levels. In addition, essential to a deep understanding of the capitalist system is the social acceptance and "approval" of the hierarchical class structure of labor and profit as a fair and just system.

The labor force in a capitalist society is significantly stratified and governed by well-defined social relations, resulting from, and resulting in, asymmetrical power relations. Fundamental within this stratification is the hierarchical division of labor and profit between those who do the work, those who oversee the work, and those who profit most from the product of the work. Resembling a pyramid, those at the "bottom" are the most dispensable, yet ironically, the most needed. Indeed, just as America needs the world's top engineers, scientists, doctors, educators, and researchers; it also needs dishwashers, janitors, fieldworkers, and laborers. Thus, in our economy, there is a need for people—a lot of people.

The dominant group in our society, in other words those who possess the greatest concentration of wealth and power at any given time, places a great demand on the country's social institutions to produce the necessary "people capital" to sustain the current system, or at the very least, not challenge it. As a result, there is a desperate need for large quantities of people to serve as laborers to continue the mass production of goods as well as to serve as consumers for the "excessive consumption of non-necessities."[5] Equally important is the need to create among the civil society the demeanor to accept social inequities as "deserved" and "just" through a belief system that gives the illusion of fairness.

In order for this process of exploitation to continue, and reproduce itself, there have to exist certain "understandings" among the general populace. These "understandings" are taught to, or forced upon, the members of the capitalist country's society via its learning institutions at both the micro and macro level, such as the school, the church, the media, etc., and via its enforcement institutions, such as the government, the police, the military, etc. In reality, however, all these institutions cannot be separated into two categories since all learning institutions contain some form of enforcement component and vice versa. Yet, for the purpose of simplifying the argument, I make a distinction here.

The inequities found in the capitalist system also have some very specific consequences for bicultural people; for it is within the bicultural community that our country placates its economic and cultural appetite to fill the most menial labor jobs in society. As a consequence, more often than not it is our bicultural parent population that is working as busboys, cooks, gardeners, fieldworkers, and in other manual labor jobs in the community. They are the ones who are working two, three, and sometimes even more jobs just to survive and feed their families. These are the people who are working without health benefits, vacation time, or worker compensation to fill those low status jobs which are looked down upon but are ultimately needed in a stratified capitalist economy. And, ironically, even when these parents do manage to move up the economic ladder to more "desirable" labor jobs, here too they are exploited. Indeed, there "is no doubt that racialized groups in the United States, especially Blacks and Latinos, are oppressed through capitalist superexploitation resulting from a segmented labor market that tends to reserve skilled, high-paying, unionized jobs for whites."[6]

The obvious consequences our bicultural parents face for working in these low-paying and physically demanding jobs is that they do not have the time or the privilege of taking time off from work to visit their children's schools; they do not have the liberty to decide their work schedules so that they are able to attend school sponsored functions; they do not have the resources to provide their children with supplemental learning experiences that are valued by the school; and they do not receive the social status and respect that is given to those individuals fortunate enough to occupy high-paying white-collar jobs. These are just some of the realities that many of our bicultural parents face for being of low socioeconomic standing *and* nonwhite.

One would wonder that given the social contradiction of the vastly unequal distribution of wealth in our country and the increasingly high percentage of people living in poverty, why aren't more people up in arms about this inequality? Why aren't people taking to the streets, challenging the current system? Why aren't people holding the wealthy and the power holders and policymakers accountable to the needs of the greater society? Why aren't we asking why the same group of people always end up at the bottom of the capitalist ladder? Why are we not perturbed by the fact that in our country poverty is not a random class consequence but rather a generational likelihood? Well, the answer to these questions, at least partially, is in the paragraphs that follow.

Perhaps the most troubling aspect of the current capitalist system, aside from the obvious exploitation factor, is how the masses so readily accept its current form as a just and fair system. That is, the advocates of our economic system are very able to legitimize the great unequal distribution of wealth and power by placing the blame on an individual's or group's merit and usefulness to the needs of the society, as cited in the argument below:

> Capitalism allows for great inequality in incomes, but it is also profoundly egalitarian. Its institutions protect the equal rights of consumers and producers, deny privilege and authority to the powerful few, and distribute wealth based on each participant's contribution to satisfying the needs of others. Everyone, therefore, should be better off in a capitalist society.[7]

To promote this belief of fairness, the capitalist system is based on the principles of meritocracy and equal opportunity, the beliefs that educational and social success is solely achieved through intelligence, diligence, creativity, and hard work and that *everybody* has an equal chance to be rich and successful. Those who fail within this system have only themselves to blame, as noted in the following passage which seeks to defend the growing unequal distribution of wealth in our society:

> Since the 1970s, Gini ratios have risen slightly in the United States, meaning incomes are becoming less equal over time. But Fogel[8] attributes most of the rise in inequality to higher-income workers putting in more hours of work, while lower-income workers reported working fewer hours. To the small extent that the rich got richer faster than the poor during the last two decades of the twentieth century, it was largely because the poor chose to work fewer hours when they could afford the basic necessities of life, whereas middle- and upper-income workers chose to continue working and reaped rewards for doing so.[9]

The fact that anybody believes this argument as the reason for the unequal distribution of wealth in our country boggles *my* mind. However, the disheartening truth is that the vast majority of our citizenry does, including those low-income workers referred to in this passage! Yet, why is that so? Why do people repeatedly allow themselves to be shortchanged and continue to fight and vote against their best interests? I will attempt to shed some light on these questions in the next section.

Hegemony

How readily people are convinced that the current mode of capitalism is fair and that we live in a system of meritocracy and equal opportunity is possible via the concept critical theorists call hegemony. Hegemony is the concealed power the ruling class has over the masses to not only convince them that the current system is fair, legitimate, and commonsensical, but also to have them support and defend the continuation of the status quo. Feinberg and Soltis state that hegemony "exists when one class controls the thinking of another class through such cultural forms as the media, the church, or the schools."[10]

Italian philosopher Antonio Gramsci was the first to put forward the concept of hegemony in his analysis of how those in power are able to win the consent of the masses and lead them in a direction that is often entirely against their benefit. He argued that the ruling class is able to coerce and sway the masses toward the elite's point of view through social practices that appear consensual and fair but in actuality benefit the very people in power. The masses participate in these "practices" because they have little power to fight them and because they have come to believe that the ideas of their social "betters" are superior to their own, or as Gramsci writes: "this consent is 'historically' caused by the prestige (and consequent confidence) which the dominant group enjoys because of its position and function in the world of production."[11]

In the school setting, this concept of hegemony is often demonstrated when parents and teachers scramble to put in place policies and decisions made by administrators and bureaucrats "for students in schools from which they are exceedingly detached,"[12] not because they are in the best interest of the students but because these orders come from people of power and prestige. This "hegemonic status"[13] also works to the advantage of the school personnel as they exercise their power over low social class parents, convincing them that their child's failure is not due to the school's or possibly the teacher's inadequacies but due to the parents' failure to support the school's sincere efforts.

A theoretical conceptualization of social control and regulation of the masses must therefore be placed within a two-prong approach: one which acknowledges the overt use of physical and/or economic power or force as a means of control and another which implies a more cloaked approach in which the dominant group leads the masses through more concealed and formative means, the latter which is often more valuable for one "can preserve control through physical or economic coercion, but naked power is far more effective cloaked in beliefs that make it appear legitimate."[14]

The societal analysis provided in this chapter is important for our discussion in that it forces a shift in thinking from viewing the relationship between bicultural parents and the public school system as consisting exclusively of internal tensions and contradiction, as in restricted to the school setting, to include external ones as well. This structural lens thus provides an umbrella framework for studying not only the tensions and contradictions found within the relationship between bicultural parents and the schools but also those found between subordinate bicultural communities and an exploitive and racist society of which education is only a part. Moreover, our discussion on hegemony brings forth the idea that social control is not always explicit or apparent, rather it functions implicitly through those very institutions which we have learned to view as neutral and fair. Thus, this line of reasoning forces us to view social institutions, such as the school system, as part of a broader framework of tension, contradictions, and conflict.

An Institutional Analysis

An institutional analysis of the United States' education system is a complex task given the varying schools of thought regarding the function of public schooling in the U.S.[15] Everybody has their own belief of what the role of the school system should be in our society in regard to educating and preparing our future workforce and leaders. The only general consensus appears to be that the public school system should function to prepare students for their future integration into civic society. That is, the schools should provide the service of preparing children for future incorporation into the American social order. A question I pose, however, is how can schools actually prepare *all* students for equal participation in a society that is inherently unequal? We live in a hierarchical society. That is obvious. So how do schools actually function to prepare students to fit into their respective tiers of society and how is this legitimized? In other words, what practices (assumptions) found within the structure of public education function to reproduce the *structure of dominance*[16] that we have in place, and how do they affect the relationship bicultural parents have with the public education system?

Social institutions, such as the church, the media, government agencies, the public school system, etc., serve to validate, legitimize, disseminate, and enforce the ideologies, values, and interests of the dominant group in society. They become the vehicle through which the populace is socialized into the existing social order and through which society acts collectively. They teach individuals what to believe and how to act to become effective members of their society rather than burdens. They also serve to identify those who dare challenge the existing social order and punish those who disrupt it.

Social institutions do not reflect all of the values and interests of all the cultural groups found in a particular society; rather they reflect those of the dominant group. These values and worldviews thus become the norm, legitimized through accepted social practices in institutional settings and taught to society's members by their agents. In the United States, the public school system has traditionally been at the forefront of this function. To be sure, American schools have always been one of the most effective tools for carrying out the will of the dominant culture in relation to its needs. The United States' schools have historically and efficiently answered the call of their country when it has needed them. They have been on the front lines of the Americanization process of immigrant children, particularly in regard to language; they taught children the dangers of communism during the Cold War era; and they have legitimized the status quo and the dominant cultural capital as an indicator of success. Historically, however, the general populace has given little attention to, or in general has agreed with, schools participating in the "necessary" function of reproducing the inequities of our society as well.

Institutional Myths

Socioeconomic and historical factors influence the everyday interactions between students, parents, administrators, and teachers in the school system through educational assumptions and myths that perpetuate the underachievement of subordinate bicultural communities.[17] Of the educational practices most detrimental to bicultural students, the following are the most commonly cited: standardized testing; tracking (placing "smart" students in Gifted and Talented Education classes and "dumb" ones in vocational trainings); the Eurocentric curriculum; differentiated teacher/school expectations for low-income students and students of color; and coercive power relations.[18] These "expressions of dominance" function under four prevailing myths regarding the institution of public education, which I challenge:

1. That public education is a meritocracy.
2. That *everyone* has an equal opportunity in education to succeed.
3. That the public schools prepare *all* students equally for participation in civic life and the work force (e.g., the Great Equalizer).
4. That the public schools are neutral, value-free, institutions of learning.

As I mentioned earlier in this chapter, the function of the meritocracy principle is to support the popular "belief [of] upward mobility, based on the premise of equal opportunity and selection by merit rather than ascriptive criteria."[19] Within the institution of education this belief holds that academic and social success is entirely contingent upon individual merit and talent. The meritocracy principle benefits our country in terms of stability in that the working class and the poor become convinced that their position in society is due to their lack of effort or talent and not due to an unfair system that is rigged in favor of the rich and the ruling class. In the school system, the meritocracy principle is played out when teachers and administrators convince bicultural parents and their children that the primary reason they are failing is due to their lack of effort and cultural capital (i.e., their "inability" to speak English) as well as the parents' lack of formal education and white-collar skills. This is often seen in schools with large Spanish-speaking populations when teachers and administrators try to convince the parents that they must speak more English to their children if they are to succeed in education or in low-income communities where teachers assume parents are not spending enough time with their children by choice rather than due to work obligations.

Missing from the logic of meritocracy, however, is the fact that many of our bicultural children attend the poorest performing schools with the lowest expectations, in the poorest and most dangerous neighborhoods. There is no equal opportunity to success. That concept is contradictory to what is really happening in the public school system and society in general. These children attend schools that have neither the qualified teaching staff (often due to turnover or burnout) nor the resources to provide the students a topnotch education. Meanwhile, their parents are busy working, sustaining the capitalist system of exploitation via their labor for "the benefit and enjoyment of a privileged few"[20] and are unable to advocate and demand what their children are rightfully entitled to: a fair and just education.

And even if the schools did provide these children with an exceptional education, where would they go? The fact is that a vast majority of our students "were never meant to have access to dominant political and economic spheres."[21] Our country is simply not capable of sustaining a high number of "qualified" individuals. A capitalist system does not allow for *everyone* to have a prosperous future. A surplus of highly qualified Latinos and Blacks would merely provide the bosses with more powerful tools of exploitation: the ability to lower wages even more based on the low demand for qualified workers, and the ability to fire workers more effortlessly given the excess of skilled workers produced by the school system.

The fact is that the school system is not a value-free, sterile institution but rather a system of social reproduction which has functioned to maintain, reproduce, and legitimize the inequities of our society. Bowles and Gintis, for example, put forward that the function of education "is the legitimation [sic] of preexisting economic disparities."[22] They specifically argue that the "educational system is an integral element in the reproduction of the prevailing class structure of society." Thus, accordingly, the institution of education is robustly influenced by the social order, above all "by the structure of dominance in society, [and] particularly [by] economic dominance."[23]

Capitalist concepts of meritocracy, authority, power, and class which provide the justification for the unequal distribution of rewards and privileges in our society as well as punitive results have also developed into "natural" educational regulation mechanisms for individuals from subordinate groups. Therefore, if there is some general agreement that bicultural residents of the United States, both immigrant and native-born alike, tend to occupy the lower socioeconomic positions of American society, either by accident or by "intent," it would stand to reason that they and their children do the same within the country's public schools.

The task ahead of us now lies in tying the structural and institutional analyses presented hitherto to the issue we have at hand: the low level of parent involvement among low-income and bicultural parents in the public school system and the low level of academic performance of their children. Indeed, while I have shared some examples above, the reader might still be asking how this chapter's critique of capitalism directly (or even indirectly) relates to parent involvement.

Well, first, a structural analysis forces us to view the problems found within the U.S. education system contextually, thus "social structures become an important analytical component in the understanding of [educational and social inequality."[24] This means we cast a critical lens on the socioeconomic structure of society which all too often has functioned to socialize and marginalize the masses rather than include them. Secondly, a structural analysis helps us explain why social intuitions (such as schools, for example) are oriented in such a way that the poor and low-income are viewed as incompetent and the source of their own inadequacies. And third, the structural analysis provides a focus for looking at how certain members of subordinate groups respond to the inequities promulgated by social institutions and how these institutions treat them when these groups begin to challenge the current system.

Let's take one more look at the above issues in more detail as we look at the relationship between the public school system and low-income parents.

A Structural Analysis of Low-income Parents in the Schools

There are consistent findings among education researchers that the majority of low-income bicultural parents hold equally high academic aspirations for their children as middle- and upper-class white parents. Moreover, they are equally interested in participating at their children's schools and being involved in their academic affairs. "The range of roles parents choose [or are allotted] for their participation in their children's schooling depends in part on their social status," however.[25] That is, these parents may either have certain barriers (often due to work obligations) that preclude them from being a greater presence at the school or they are assigned low impact labor chores (such as cutting papers, making copies, checking off homework, etc.) when they *do* show up, often based on the school personnel's assumption that these parents are incapable of doing more meaningful activities.

This is not meant to imply, however, that the manual tasks mentioned here are not of value to the overworked teacher. As a former classroom teacher, I know that this is valuable support. Rather, I bring these jobs forth because often these are the *only* tasks bicultural parents are *allowed* to perform and because these tasks form the foundation of what the vast majority of our educators want these parents to do when they visit the schools. In other words, this is what is *expected* of low-income, bicultural parents: their participation in the labor sense.

I made an earlier argument that it is disingenuous to believe that parents who live disempowered in society will be treated as empowered individuals, or even as equals, in the school system; a phenomenon which has most often been studied under the examination of teachers' attitudes about, and expectations for, low-income children or children of color. It has been suggested, for example, that teachers' interactions and behaviors with particular groups of students vary according to the attributes that the students or their parents possess.

School personnel attach values to the social, economic, and cultural capital that parents and children bring to the school and these affect the quality of their relationship with them. The findings of most of these studies have been that teachers and school personnel act more favorably toward students and families who are middle-class or upper-class and white.[26]

The power of the school to legitimize certain displays of social, cultural, and economic capital is therefore reflected in the interpersonal relationships between school personnel and bicultural parents. White, affluent parents are automatically bestowed high levels of social and cultural capital, thus when they have questions or concerns they are treated as social equals, if not "betters," by school personnel. Low-income bicultural parents, on the other hand, are viewed and treated as social inferiors and they are challenged and rebuffed when they have a concern. All too often low-income parents have their questions about school-related matters or complaints about personnel "neutralized by the teachers' [and administrators'] superior status."[27] Thus, it appears quite apparent that parents' social class determines the quality of their participation at their children's school, and this is most evident in the unequal treatment low-income parents receive, regardless of race, when they have school-related concerns or issues.

Negative school interactions between school personnel and low-income parents warrant that the issue of the latter's low level of school participation be viewed within the socioeconomic context presented earlier in this chapter. School personnel exercise what Shannon refers to as "hegemonic status," which is a "dominant and silencing status [that] is sustained by society accepting the status quo."[28] Thus for teachers and school personnel, low-status parents do not deserve the attention high-status parents are afforded since, in the eyes of the school staff, poor parents are of no real threat to them. This is validated according to the concept of meritocracy since it is believed that low-income parents *must* be lacking in something, which is why they are living in poverty in the first place and their children are doing poorly academically.

Being of low income is debilitating in our society, particularly since poverty in our country is associated with lack of effort and intelligence. Within this context, poverty and low social class are viewed to be cured by "fixing" the individual or the group who "possesses" these qualities through institutional interventions. William

Ryan, in his class book *Blaming the Victim* described the process in the following manner:

> In education, we have programs of 'compensatory education' to build up the skills and attitudes of the ghetto child, rather than structural changes in the schools. In race relations, we have social engineers who think up ways of 'strengthening' the Negro family, rather than methods of eradicating racism. In health care, we develop new programs to provide health information (to correct the supposed ignorance of the poor) and to reach out and discover cases of untreated illness and disability (to compensate for their supposed unwillingness to seek treatment). Meanwhile the gross inequalities of our medical care delivery systems are left completely unchanged. As we might expect, the logical outcome of analyzing social problems in terms of deficiencies of the victims is the development of programs aided at correcting those deficiencies. The formula for action becomes extraordinarily simple: change the victim.[29]

Suffice it to say in this chapter that blaming the victim is a common institutional response to the inequities of our society, inequities which have their root in the socioeconomic structure of our social order. Moreover, by blaming the victim, institutions serve an important function in not only diverting attention from the dominant groups' social and economic practices, but also in socializing both the dominant and the subordinate groups into maintaining the status quo, thus neutralizing the potential for change.

As I conclude this chapter, below is the first critical incident that the reader is urged to read and reflect upon. The questions for discussion will help you think about the contents of this chapter as well.

Critical Incident

Countryside Elementary is an urban neighborhood school which has seen significant demographic and economic changes during the last fifteen years. Once predominantly middle-class and white, the neighborhood has shifted to being predominantly working-class and ethnically diverse.

Mrs. Jeffries has been teaching 2nd grade at Countryside Elementary for over 20 years. While Mrs. Jeffries still generally enjoys her job with the children, the last few years she has been overheard in the teachers' lounge lamenting about how "values have changed" since she first started teaching at the school and how the children appear to be "getting worse every year," including the parents.

One particular day Mrs. Jeffries calls the mother of Louise Willis, a student in her class who is performing significantly behind grade level, for an impromptu parent conference to discuss her concerns. At the meeting, Mrs. Jeffries tells Mrs. Willis that Louise is significantly behind in all content areas and that she often comes to school unprepared and without homework. She also tells her that if Louise's academic work and effort do not improve she will have no other option but to keep her in the 2nd grade.

Mrs. Willis understands Mrs. Jeffries' concerns and apologetically explains to her that she is a single mother working two jobs to make ends meet so she does not always have the time to supervise her daughter's school work. To this, Mrs. Jeffries responds by telling her that perhaps she should put Louise higher up on her list of responsibilities because she as the teacher can only do so much in the classroom. "Sure, work is important," says Mrs. Jeffries, "but so is your daughter's future." Mrs. Jeffries needs her support at home so that Louise understands at an early age the importance of an education so that she can be successful in life. After all, Mrs. Jeffries argues, she wouldn't want Louise to follow in her footsteps of having such a hard work life, would she? Some sacrifices on Mrs. Willis' part now could go a long way for Louise's future, Mrs. Jeffries continues.

Mrs. Willis agrees with Mrs. Jeffries and promises that she will attempt to pay closer attention to Louise's school work and will try to maintain closer contact with her so as to avoid future misunderstandings. She leaves the meeting just in time to arrive on time to her evening job.

Questions for Reflection
1. What assumptions is Mrs. Jeffries making about Mrs. Willis' attempt to help her daughter?
2. Is Mrs. Jeffries' assessment of the situation correct?
3. Do Mrs. Jeffries' solutions for Louise's academic problems seem appropriate?
4. What other solutions can be proposed to help Mrs. Willis' child?

5. What factors affect Mrs. Willis' ability to help her child in school? Are these individual factors, institutional factors, or structural factors?

Racism and Deficit Thinking

Employing structural economic discrimination theories to examine the relationship between the dominant culture and subordinate groups is very useful for recognizing assumptions and practices which function within institutions to preclude an authentic relationship between the two. Yet despite their usefulness, these frameworks are not enough to completely clarify the relationship between bicultural parents and the institution of public education. For lacking within most socioeconomic oriented frameworks are "cross cutting cleavages of race and gender."[1] That is, if we exclusively use structural economic oriented approaches for understanding the relationship between the public school system and low-income bicultural parents, we tend "to limit, if not totally negate, the objective situation of racial and ethnic prejudice that leads to racial discrimination."[2]

Most economic exploitation frameworks establish the private ownership of the means of production (land, resources, and capital), occupational position, and caste as the major foundations for inequality in America.[3] The primary feature for differentiating peoples' struggles within industrial societies thus stems from access to, and power and status derived from, economic resources and wealth. In other words these frameworks propose that "economic conditions are at the center of human activity [and] other activities and beliefs, including education, are in some sense *determined* by economic conditions."[4]

Notwithstanding the compelling economic exploitation arguments proposed in these frameworks, I find it particularly difficult to be convinced that solely class divisions can explain the inauthentic relationship that exists between bicultural parents and the public schools and that these divisions supercede all "other kinds of divisions, including those based on race and ethnicity."[5] And while I do believe that racism has its foundation and function in economic exploitation, the historical trajectory of race relations in our country has greatly influenced how nonwhites are currently perceived and treated in contemporary society. Therefore, whether racism is institutionalized, embedded, or entrenched,[6] race relations are an important area of study as we search for an explanation for the poor relationship between bicultural parents and the public schools.

We must therefore critically examine race relations within our country and how these have been played out in the relationship between the agents of American institutions and nonwhites. This added component of an analysis of race and ethnic relations to the structural perspective is important in that it challenges us to look at poor educational outcomes and poor school/community relationships for specific bicultural social groups as not simply the results of economic factors. We are challenged to consider these issues as a product of the socioeconomic *and* racial histories of our nation, or more specifically, the systems of capitalism *and* white supremacy.

Racism and Race Relations

Racism in our nation is not always obvious. Yes, we have the Ku Klux Klan, media stereotypes, racial profiling, hate crimes, and immigrant bashing. Yet, there are many more subtle hidden manifestations of racial discrimination which despite laws to prohibit it continue to operate in every facet of our lives. This form of racism is that which is "institutionalized," implanted within the structure of our society and reflected in the everyday interactions between human beings. This racism is prevalent and ingrained in our society and cannot be ignored when talking about the relationship between school personnel and nonwhite parents.

Racism in our country is complex. It is denied by many whites in the United States yet experienced by many nonwhites. It is challenged in the courts by many nonwhites yet it is ignored or denied when witnessed by many whites. It is taboo in the public opinion of many white Americans, yet it is hegemonic in that it is reproduced in the public's psyche without much resistance, in both whites and nonwhites. Moreover, racism is seen as a nasty chapter in our history with examples pointing to the enslavement of Blacks and the genocide of the American Indians, yet it is still an everyday way of life in our country, a pillar of our social structure and its institutions.

Cintron explains this institutionalized racism in the following manner:

Racism in its most subtle, its most complex, its most stubborn and, thereby, its most insidious form, is racism which is institutional. As part of the thinking of Americans, racial prejudice has been much analyzed and much condemned. As part of the institutional life of America, racism has been too little understood and too often overlooked. But it is not just prejudiced individuals who are pushing our nation toward two societies . . . It is the overwhelming difficulty of controlling our own institutions which, being a product of history, cannot but perpetuate practices which advantage the typical white and penalize the typical black.[7]

To position the source of racism within America's institutional structures is to shift a significant part of the responsibility away from viewing racism as solely an individual or group act. In other words, racism is not seen as an exclusive trait of certain individuals from the "Deep South" or members of the Ku Klux Klan but rather it is understood as an American institutional way of life that permeates the daily relationships between whites and nonwhites. Darder explains the functioning of this form of racism:

Institutional racism is a form of racial discrimination that is woven into the fabric of the power relations, social arrangements, and practice through which collective actions result in the use of race as a criterion to determine who is rewarded in society.[8]

Institutional racism therefore does not just function to put people of color at a disadvantage in our society; it also implicitly functions to put whites at an overall *advantage* in our social structure and in power relations. In schools this advantage comes in the form of education being tailored to fit the middle- and upper-class white student, creating "an education pipeline that is often inaccessible to low-income ethnic-minority students, including those who are limited-English-proficient."[9]

Institutional racism, however, continues to be overlooked by policymakers and school personnel as one of the primary sources of inequality in our society, despite the fact that it dominates virtually every aspect of our social and private lives. It is part of who we are as a nation and is represented daily in how we conduct our everyday business. Institutional racism, while most clearly seen in the under-representation of people of color in positions of power, is fundamentally also seen in the centrality of whiteness in our country. This white-centered society is best described by the white populations' greater access to our country's power structures, greater ownership and control of its resources, and the ability to enforce its values and worldview as the norm.

This "rightness of whiteness" which is prevalent in our nation is also characterized by the inability of whites to see their position of privilege.[10] Peggy McIntosh likens this white privilege to an "invisible package of unearned assets which . . . can be cashed in each day, but about which [whites are] meant to remain oblivious."[11] This unearned advantage which largely remains unseen by whites, however, is often quite obvious to people of color who develop multiple manners to negotiate their existence in a white-centered society.[12] It is also obvious in the school setting, particularly in the underachievement of bicultural students and the often negative relationship between school personnel and nonwhite students and parents.

Using a "foundational" and institutional racism lens, Núñez, for example, argues that the low academic achievement of bicultural students and the exclusion of their parents from the public school system can best be examined using what he calls an "embedded racism" framework. The focus of this framework is the interpersonal relationships between school personnel and parents of color and the subtle forms of racism that are included in their exchanges. He writes the following:

> Institutional racism, originating in historically unequal relations be-tween whites and nonwhites in the United States permeates Ameri-can social institutions. Embedded racism is the manifestation of institutional racism in individuals. It is a form of subtle, unconscious racial prejudice that emerges in the well-intentioned relations be-tween teachers and students, between school and home and between dominant society and subordinate communities. It emerges in [the educators'] honest attempts to help children. Their attempts, how-ever, colored by cultural and historical myths, manifest themselves in low expectations of culturally diverse children. It is based in the belief that culturally diverse communities are deficient in one way or another and must be provided compensation to make up for these deficiencies.[13]

Because racism manifests itself through a complex series of unconscious and unseen networks of interpersonal relationships between whites and nonwhites, it is not always intentional or obvious. Instead, racism can be restrained and unobtrusive, particularly to whites. And for the vast majority of America's teachers and administrators, their relationship with nonwhite parents is tainted by this embedded racism which is bound within a frame of reference which views low-income, bicultural children and their parents as deprived or lacking. This view is founded on commonly accepted, albeit biased, theories of human development and potential. These theories of development are rooted in "a systemic conception of inherent and natural inferiority, which emerged in the late seventeenth or early eighteenth century and culminated in the nineteenth century when it acquired the pseudoscientific reinforcement of *biological* theories of race."[14]

Theoretical Perspectives on Race and Inferiority

Deficit theories form the foundation for both conservative and liberal-leaning social scientists and policymakers who attempt to explicate why certain racial and ethnic groups fail academically, economically, and socially at higher rates than the dominant group in society. These explanations draw the conclusion that the primary blame for academic underachievement and social maladjustment should be placed on the social group in question. In other words, the source of inequality is not seen as being located within the dominant social structure, from which the dominant white middle- and upper-class population benefits most, but rather within the bicultural and/or low-income individual and his/her group.

In American society, deficit theories (influenced by deficit thinking) have served a fundamental role in explaining the academic and social underachievement of bicultural students, their parents, and their communities.[15] These deficit theories work like this: (1) There exists a disadvantaged group; (2) it is alleged that the cause of their disadvantage lies within the group itself; (3) "the culture is the likely source of this cause; (4) let us see what we can find in their cultural attributes that would explain their disadvantaged status."[16] Thus, through these deficit theories it has been argued repeatedly that students, particularly those who are "low-SES and of color, fail in school because they and their families have internal defects, or deficits, that thwart the learning process."[17] These theories form a triad of deficiency explanations posited within the bicultural child and family: deficiency in genetics, deficiency in environment, and deficiency in culture. Explicit in these theories is the attempt to legitimize failure within the bicultural family; implicit is their function as an expression of dominance and superiority for the dominant, white culture. The most well known deficit theories can be identified in the three basic categories:

(1) *Biological Deficit Theories*: This category includes the "classic racist theories . . . in which racial inequality [is] attributed to genetic and thus hereditary inferiority on the part of certain races."[18] These theories maintain that specific races (i.e., nonwhites) tend to occupy subordinate roles in any society due to their inherent and biological disadvantages, specifically in the area of intelligence.[19] This is often "proven" by pointing to the lower performance of nonwhites on standardized achievement tests or intelligence tests.

These sorts of theories are often associated with more politically and socially conservative sectors of our society who espouse a more functionalist view of school and society.[20] It represents a form of Darwinist thinking in which it is argued that the stronger (mentally and genetically) "survive" and earn the power to dominate over subordinate groups due to their innate superiority. And, interestingly enough, while at times these theories appear to fall out of favor within the area of academe, they continue to reappear even in the most recent of writings in the social sciences, thus their influence cannot be underestimated.[21]

(2) *Structural or Environmental Deficit Theories*: These theories also emphasize weaknesses found in the bicultural racial groups in question. Those who support these theories tend to come from a more liberal political orientation, however. They, in a sense, contend that historical factors such as slavery and long periods of discrimination have created weak structures among the families and individuals of these bicultural groups, as well as other deficiencies. The presence of these "handicaps" in these groups have led those who advocate this view to propose more government intervention in the personal lives

of the "disadvantaged" or "deprived." Evidence of this has been seen socially in the welfare system and educationally in compensatory education programs such as transitional bilingual education, Head Start, and Upward Bound. Thus the goal of these programs is to provide the "disadvantaged" with a "more positive" and "more supportive" environment than they may otherwise be exposed to in their low-income neighborhood or family.

A significant critique of structural/environmental deficit theories should be focused on the underlying belief found in these "well-intentioned" programs which places the sole burden of the blame for poor academic and social achievement in the lap of the subordinate groups rather than on the existing social structure. Specifically, within these environmental deficit theories, there is the underlying belief that the current socio-political system is fair and just and that the subordinate groups merely need a "step up" to effectively participate and reap the rewards society has to offer.

(3) *Cultural Deficit Theories*: Although often used in conjunction with the structural deficit theories mentioned above, this category's emphasis is "on attitudes and values rather than on social structure," specifically the "cultural characteristics" of low ambition, emotional instability, low self-esteem, lack of discipline, etc. The work of Edward Banfield and his "culture of poverty" is a good illustration of this line of reasoning. Banfield, for example, argues that:

> Inequality in the United States is largely attributable to a 'lower class culture,' consisting of such traits as a present rather than future orientation, a lack of work discipline, and so on. Individuals who share this 'culture' do poorly in school, and their low educational attainment creates conditions of poverty and powerlessness, which interact with each other and create a vicious circle to perpetuate educational inequalities.[22]

Fundamentally similar is the work of Peter Skerry who argues that the Mexican-Americans' heavy reliance on Spanish, weak institutional ties, folk beliefs and superstitions, ambivalence, machismo, humility, and deference to authority, etc. all contribute to their subordinate status.[23] He views the Mexican family and the Mexican culture as a significant barrier to upward mobility and his work reflects the traditional perceptions of the bicultural family as pathological and its own worst enemy. He further maintains that Latino children will need well-funded and well-managed programs to help them overcome their cultural obstacles.

A basic underlying assumption found within this category of theories is the belief "which suggests that only those experiences provided by Anglo middle-class culture can provide the basis for school preparedness" and upward social mobility.[24] And while there may be some truth to this statement, it is not due to the fact that bicultural families do not have anything of value to offer their children but rather because American society places greater worth on the cultural and social capital of middle- and upper-class whites.

By critically analyzing the underlying ideology behind these deficit theories, we can therefore conclude that they serve numerous purposes:

1. By finding the deficiency within the bicultural group under scrutiny, the dominant culture is able to "explain away" virtually any social problem in existence, particularly when this social problem contradicts the beliefs and ideologies on which the country in question are founded on and from which this group benefits most.
2. By imposing unsubstantiated biological, cultural, and social pathologies on bicultural groups, the dominant culture is able to substantiate and legitimize the withholding of many basic human rights (i.e., cultural and linguistic rights, equal opportunity to make a living, equal educational opportunities, etc.) without guilt, and
3. By viewing bicultural individuals and groups as deficient, the dominant culture is able to elevate itself to a position of superiority over the bicultural populace, thus justifying (again without guilt) economic and social domination and its punitive results.

It is under these dominant biases against bicultural communities that the deficit theories have been used by the public schools to identify the role of the bicultural family in education and explain their children's lack of academic achievement. Indeed, contemporary parental influence assumptions and the public school system's perception about bicultural parents are still heavily influenced by deficit thinking, and this is part of the reason why bicultural parents are frequently subjected to parent involvement practices that are primarily designed to change or "educate" them. Understanding these theories also helps explain why bicultural parents are often exclusively blamed for their children's academic shortcoming and how the school system is able to easily alleviate itself of its important educational responsibilities. This sentiment is echoed by Cummins, who writes:

> This form of discourse defines culturally diverse students and parents as inferior in various ways and therefore responsible for their own school failure and poverty. It also takes the focus of critical scrutiny away from the school and society. In this way, the educational and social status quo is legitimated and pressures for change are deflected.[25]

The evolution of deficit theories and the unequal treatment of people of color in relation to whites function to legitimize racial discrimination and are the product of white prejudice and white supremacy. Thus, a clear understanding of the problems facing bicultural students and parents must "examine issues of race, ethnicity, income, deficit mentality, and ideologies . . . especially that of *White supremacy.*"[26]

Therefore, a faithful analysis of issues related to the traditional educational "failure" of bicultural students must be historic in nature on two fronts. First, it must take into account the historical processes that have contributed to the creation of an asymmetrical power relationship between white America and people of color, particularly Latinos and African-Americans, in relation to the development of capitalism. And secondly, this analysis must include a study of the relationship between whites and nonwhites within a context of white supremacy. Thus, for our purposes, we need to begin to understand how these concepts are manifested within the school setting and what educators can do so as to avoid common pitfalls that make their relationship with bicultural parents inauthentic and oppressive.

In summary, I argue that that our socioeconomic system has a strong hold on our public education system because "schools are institutions that respond to and reflect the larger society."[27] Using a structural perspective, I contend that schools use universally unquestioned educational practices based on the need to sustain and replicate the status quo in terms of economics and race. More specifically, I argue that many institutional practices are closely related to the institutionalized and embedded racism outlined in this chapter and the economic exploitation factors outlined in the previous one.

For the remainder of this chapter I would like to tie the race relations argument more closely to school practices that affect nonwhite parents. To do this, I pose the following questions for the reader to reflect on and to guide our discussion:

1. How is racism manifested against bicultural children and their parents?
2. Does one need to use specific racial epithets to be considered a racist?
3. What purpose does it serve the school system to deny bicultural parents a voice in their children's education?
4. How do the schools relate to parents who are nonwhite, and how do these parents relate to them in a racist institution such as education?

Specific Issues Regarding Racism in the Public Schools

It is "not surprising that racism and discrimination find their way into schools in much the same way that they find their way into other institutions."[28] For some, this proposition is bold: racism permeates all the institutions that form the foundation of our country, including the institution of education. Those with doubts may ask themselves, how can racism survive in the school system? Aren't all teachers and school personnel liberal in their thinking and overall accepting of all their students and their parents? Wouldn't a racist educator be easily identified and singled out for the good of the students?

Well, I would respond that the problem with racism in the school setting is that its manifestations are not always done with harm intended or by people who consider themselves racist. No, rather racial discrimination is often committed under "good intentions" by individuals who unknowingly use a racist lens to view their bicultural students and their parents.[29] Moreover, racial discrimination against people of color is not always exclusively committed by whites. On the contrary, it is often just as easily perpetuated by nonwhite school personnel who accept the dominant form of thinking as the norm and view the nonwhite parents through a deficit lens.

The social construction of race manifests itself in ways that schools structure inequalities around it.[30] These inequalities then work to determine the limitations placed upon students' opportunities to learn, to have access to the academic curriculum, and to experience educational mobility. To counteract these issues Latino and African-American students and parents, as well as other bicultural parents, often take an oppositional or distanced approach to dealing with school practices. This also leaves the parent with the task of addressing problems related to their own particular child.

For example, in the education system certain pedagogical practices seen as normal and necessary by mainstream America negatively affect the academic performance of bicultural students. Students of color, for instance, may experience lower teacher expectations, differential classroom interactions, inadequate counseling, less access to pertinent information, ability grouping and tracking, disproportionate representation in special education, culturally biased curricular and instructional practices, culturally biased assessment tools, altered discipline methods, and often instruction from the least experienced or qualified teachers. These practices have all been consistent concerns of bicultural student advocates and bicultural communities in that they provide low-visibility opportunities for the dominant culture to discriminate against children and communities of color, thus legitimizing their academic underachievement. Yet these practices are frequently just as accepted by teachers and administrators of color as by whites.

At times, bicultural parents whose children have been affected by these practices respond by questioning the school personnel and their policies. This leads to mistrust about the school's practices and often results in bicultural parents distancing themselves from the school's outreach efforts. As a result, the only contact that bicultural parents have with the school is when there is either a problem with their child or when they are advocating on their behalf in light of the unjust pedagogical practices. This sort of participation thus becomes the norm as bicultural parents must constantly be vigilant that their child is not being socially and educationally harmed by the school. This struggle for educational equity becomes a constant struggle however as these parents realize that their concerns are neither warranted nor taken into consideration by the school personnel.

Differential Treatment and Paternalism

The power school personnel wield over the low-income bicultural communities they serve is what makes this deeply entrenched racism and their harmful educational practices even more insidious. Indeed, there is a debilitating intersect between race and class when low-income bicultural parents attempt to become involved in schools beyond the specified band of acceptable behaviors. This is most apparent in the treatment low-income bicultural parents receive when they try to participate in the school system beyond the low-impact activities assigned to them or when they attempt to actively advocate for their children and their community.

Lareau and Horvat argue that while "social class seems to influence how black and white parents negotiate their relationship with schools, for blacks race plays an important role, independent of social class, in framing the terms of their relationship."[31] In their study of parents from two third grade classrooms, for example, Lareau and Horvat found that Black parents not only "approached the school with open criticism" but also encountered more barriers in complying with school expectations than white parents of the same social class.

Teachers' and administrators' interactions and behaviors with particular groups of students and parents vary according to the attributes that the latter possess. There is a significant difference in how school personnel interact and treat white affluent parents as opposed to low-income, ethnically diverse parents.[32] This is most apparent in upper-class white school communities where the status and power of these parents has forced school personnel to not only "endure" their presence and "oppressive participation"[33] but also to actively seek ways of satisfying their whims.[34] Certainly, understanding that these are powerful people with sufficient time and resources, school personnel diligently work to appease these parents, often causing them to bow to capricious requests, often for fear of a lawsuit.

White affluent parents who hold power, both monetarily and in the cultural capital sense, are seen as the standard of good parenting and the foundation of their children's strong academic achievement.

The argument by many educators and policymakers appears to be that since children who come from middle- and upper-class white parents are the ones who always seem to perform best in school, these families must be doing something right. Yet, while these parents are revered for their effective parenting, they are also often seen as "over-involved [sic] and intrusive."[35] But this is tolerated since school personnel who work in schools in predominantly middle- and upper-class white communities view this parent population as their social equals, if not their superiors. Moreover, these students are pretty much destined to succeed given the financial and social status of their parents, who have the options to provide their children with tutors, supplemental learning experiences, and college and job-entry advantages.

The contrary scenario is often true, however, for low-income ethnically diverse communities. Parents in low income communities of color find themselves in what Shannon refers to as the "paradox of minority parent involvement."[36] The essence of this paradox is the no-win situation these parents are placed in. They are criticized by school personnel for their lack of involvement and low presence at the school yet actively dismissed or repressed when they demonstrate acts of advocacy or activism on behalf of their children or their community. In addition, whereas white parents are seen as the key to their children's success, ethnically diverse and low-income parents are viewed as barriers to theirs. Accordingly, the hegemonic status bestowed upon more affluent white parents and their children opens doors for them while for bicultural parents their participation is a constant struggle. This, of course, affects the nature of how these parents are involved at their children's school.

Bicultural parents live in a constant battle for their children's educational rights. Often understanding the view that the school personnel hold of them, they still build up the courage to attend important school functions and make attempts to have their voices heard. And even when bicultural parents, particularly those who are immigrants or non-English speaking, have legitimate concerns regarding the educational endeavors of the school in relation to their children's well being, they frequently refrain from challenging the school system for fear of being accused of being "out of line" or, worst yet, being disappointed through failed advocacy.

When bicultural parents do challenge the school system, for whatever reason that may be, very common and frequent barriers arise. Most notably, bicultural parents are slighted, ignored, shunned, or even humiliated by school personnel, as indicated by the following words by a Latina parent leader from San Diego:

One notices the difference. If [a Latino parent] has a problem and they send a note to the principal asking for a meeting, they never get a response. The principal doesn't reply. They don't give you a response. And that's what we noticed when we were in a particular struggle. When we would send complaints [to the principal] we'd never get a response. Then one day, one of the ladies that was with us, [well] not completely [with us] but she supported us, sent the principal a letter asking for a meeting. She's American.[37] That very same day she got a meeting. That very same day!

This comment by this Latina parent illustrates that nonwhite children and parents are cognizant of the fact that they are treated differently. They are dismissed as nuisances when they attempt to be involved in meaningful interactions with the school, while white parents are rewarded via positive interactions with school personnel and the institution of public education as a whole. In fact, not only does the school welcome middle- and upper-class white parents, but they are respected and listened to when it comes to important decision-making issues. This, however, does not go unnoticed by bicultural parents who internalize that feeling of not being wanted.

When the culture and the class of the family are different than that of the school's, well ingrained and often unrecognized thoughts of racial superiority begin to emerge. It now becomes the duty of the school to impose its wishes onto the bicultural family. Deficit projections are cast and bicultural families who wish to participate are seen as incapable of doing so and therefore rebuffed and rejected. Moreover, these parents have no real power, the school personnel reasons, so they have nothing to worry about. Eventually, these parents will tire or become discouraged and will go away (which, unfortunately, *is* often the case). This, of course, greatly affects not only the view that bicultural parents have of the school and of themselves, but the view that their children have of their parents, themselves, and their culture as demonstrated by the following comments from the Latina parent in San Diego: "That sort of treatment makes one feel bad. You know, we sent so many letters to the principal and why doesn't she sit down with us to talk about our problems and our concerns?"

Most manifestations of how bicultural parents are by all accounts treated as children are best represented in the paternalistic treatment they receive from school personnel within the school system. These parents are summarily excluded from having any authentic input into decisions that not only affect the school in general but their children in particular. In California this is most evident in the struggle over bilingual education in which countless Latino parents have reported difficulty in obtaining waivers that will allow their children to participate in these programs. The Latino parents' motives and judgments are questioned by school administrators as they are put into positions in which they must defend the decisions they make for their children.

Many researchers have documented how Spanish-speaking Latino parents are not only treated disrespectfully when they try to have meaningful participation in their children's education but how their input is minimized and disregarded by paternalistic board members and administrators who view these parents as "ungrateful" for the efforts being put forth by the school system[38]. In one statement, for example, Galindo quotes an Orange County Board of Education member who states: "I would have thought that most parents would want their children to learn English as quickly and fluently as possible, and I'm quite surprised that so many are unhappy. I think we're doing their kids a favor."[39]

Bicultural Parents' Perception about Education

Whether bicultural parents feel threatened, intimidated, or unwanted or whether school personnel actively discourage their participation, the issue remains that these parents have not been inclined to visibly participate at their children's schools in large numbers beyond well-defined limits. Therefore, in order to develop an authentic relationship with bicultural parents, in addition to understanding how school personnel respond to culturally diverse parents, it is equally important to be aware of how particular groups perceive their interactions with the schools and with school personnel. Similarly it is actions with the schools and with school personnel. Similarly it is important to recognize their personal lived experiences with the public education system.

Lareau and Horvat[40] contend, for example, that African-American parents are quite cognizant of race relations in the school system and often approach the school with distrust, particularly if they are low-income. Lopez argues that Latino parents view themselves as being quite involved in their children's education by supporting their children's educational endeavors through advice and encouragement, though this is not commonly recognized by their children's schools.[41] And finally, parents from certain Asian groups, considered to be the "model minority," appear to be more receptive to the schools' efforts due to their immigrant experiences and the value they place on formal education. That is, Asian immigrants are often willing to "accept" discrimination and prejudice in return for perceived social advancement opportunities which compared to those that were afforded to them in their native countries are quite favorable.[42]

In their study, Ritblatt, Beatty, Cronan and Ochoa[43] surveyed a total of 506 parents of school-aged children in San Diego County and came up with similar findings. Factors related to the problem of parental involvement in education were gathered from the literature after examining various theoretical models. Items included examining reasons why parents are involved in their children's education as well as why parents are *not* involved in their children's education. Additional items addressed issues directly related to individual parental situations.

The results of this study allow for certain generalizations that indicate distinct cultural groups interact differently with the school system. For example, they concluded that African-American parents tend to interact with the schools in modes of resistance given their personal experiences with the system. Moreover, African-American parents tended to have more contact with the school, as indicated by the fact that they spent more time on general school issues and on specific issues related to their child, particularly behavioral issues. However, they were also more likely to have been frustrated in some of these contacts, as indicated by their greater feeling of mystification about school matters.

The results of this study also concluded that Latino families felt more confident that the schools were sensitive to their needs, though their responses may have been more related to the cultural lens they used to view education. That is, for Latino parents, these findings may not tell the full story of their involvement with the schools. The results that point to Latinos having a positive view of the schools' ability to be sensitive and to express care may in fact be more attributed to a cultural value that places the school/teacher as a co-equal with parents in the education of children. For example, in many cases if the student has a problem, that problem may go uncontested because Latino parents feel that the school or the teacher is fulfilling their role as the responsible agent. Another finding from this study was that Latino parents initially give the schools full trust only to find abuse in the relationship. Thus, as Latino parents get more involved with the school system, their level of direct involvement with and concern about the quality of education provided to their child increases.

Other conclusions drawn from this study point to white parents tending to focus exclusively on their own children as part of their involvement with the schools and Asian parents as being guided by cultural traditions that give schools the space and authority to educate their children, thus open to collaborating with schools at a distance. In other words, Asian parents generally preferred to support their children's academic work at home.

Finally, the research of Ritblatt, Beatty, Cronan and Ochoa concludes that there is a need for research that: (1) places attention on the relationship among schools, the wider society, and the conditions that hinder or promote home-school collaboration; (2) focuses on why parents who are marginalized by race, class, and gender are less able to procure high levels of quality educational services for their children and/or access to the college bound curriculum; (3) examines culturally sensitive approaches to engaging parents in the education of their children and in school governance; and (4) examines how parent involvement can be institutionalized to support schools and facilitate better educational success for low-income children.

Summary

I have little doubt that racism and the racialization of parents by teachers and administrators play a significant role in the relationship between schools and parents in that they prevent their participation and perpetuate their exclusion. Thus, this influence is negative, tainted by the racist lens we all possess that is the product of our history as a nation of conquest against nonwhite groups, namely Blacks, Latinos, and Native Americans. All too real is the continuing existence of Manifest Destiny and the belief that bicultural communities are deficient in some way or another.

The manifestation of these negative race relations is often seen in the inauthentic relationship between school personnel and low-income and working-class nonwhite parents. This insincerity is easily recognizable in the patterns of paternalism and exclusion, and it contributes to the tensions and contradictions that underlie the relationships between whites and nonwhites. In the next chapter, I will take a closer look at three specific tensions and how they are manifested in culture, knowledge, and power and how these tensions characterize the relationship between school personnel and bicultural parents.

Critical Incident

Harris Elementary is in a low-income, racially diverse community, though the largest ethnic group is Latinos, many of whom are also English Learners. Mr. Powell, site principal of Harris Elementary, is worried because the school's standardized test scores have been declining the last few years. If this trend continues, the school will soon be open to sanctions under state and federal guidelines and he could possibly lose his job. He calls for a staff meeting early in the school year to share his concerns.

While the conversation at the meeting is civil, several of the teachers are concerned that the blame is being misplaced. They argue that they are doing their best in the classroom and suggest that the parents are not doing their part in educating their children. Mr. Kane, a new teacher at the site, speaks up by saying that the staff must make efforts to "educate the parents so that they understand how important an education is nowadays." Mrs. Reyes, a veteran teacher, supports Mr. Kane's position and adds that the parents also need to be taught how to interact with their children so that they have more "cognitive stimulation" at home. She continues by stating that there is a need to stress to the parents that education is not an easy thing to acquire and that it requires hard work. She sums up her comments by saying that the parents should do more to help their children at home. "They need to learn to say 'no' and turn off the TV," she concludes. To this, Mr. Harvey, another veteran teacher, adds that efforts must also be made to teach the parents how to read and write in English. "Many of them are illiterate in their own language, so how can they be expected to help their children at home?" he concludes.

Questions for Reflection

1. What assumptions are being made about bicultural parents and children at this meeting?
2. Are the staff members' assumptions correct?
3. Are the teachers' comments reflective of "deficit thinking" and/or "racism"? If so, give examples.
4. What alternative motives and/or factors could be influencing the students' academic achievement and their parents' participation at the school?
5. What solutions do you suppose the teachers will propose to improve their school's test scores?
6. What would you add to this discussion if you were at the meeting?

Culture, Knowledge, and Power

Navigating the school campus is no easy task, for teachers or parents. Teachers and administrators have a lot to deal with during the course of the day, with their interactions with parents being one of the most important and necessary tasks. These daily interactions oftentimes become burdensome chores, however, when they turn out negative or hostile, leaving the teacher or the principal to wonder what happened and what they can do in the future to make the parents "happy." For parents, particularly low-income bicultural parents, navigating the school campus can equally be a troublesome task, especially when they go to the school in search of an answer to a burning question or to resolve an issue regarding their child but return home disappointed or dismayed. It is in these instances, where both parties are well-intentioned and equally frustrated, that we find the presence of underlying tensions in the relationship between bicultural parents and school personnel.

Most school personnel tend to view their relationship with parents as distant and professional, void of biases, and always in the "best interest" of children. In their work, Lareau and Horvat found that educators for the most part felt "that they enthusiastically welcomed parental involvement and believed that their requests for parental involvement were neutral, technically efficient, and designed to promote higher levels of achievement."[1] These authors concluded, however, that most teachers in reality "selected from a narrow band of acceptable behaviors" for parents as demonstrations of involvement, preferring that they be accepting and non-judgmental of the teachers' and the schools' practices.

The truth of the matter is that the relationship between bicultural parents and school personnel is not neutral or sterile. Rather, this relationship is rife with contradictions and tensions, deeply influenced by a broader set of issues that define all relationships in our society between dominant and subordinate social groups. At the root of these school-centered tensions between bicultural parents and school personnel, I argue, are societal contradictions and tensions in the area of economic exploitation and race relations which cannot be ignored (concepts which were explored in greater detail in the two previous chapters).

Ochoa believes that tensions at the schools arise "as [bicultural] parents assert their rights as advocates for their children and their communities."[2] I am in complete agreement with that position. However, I add that tensions between bicultural parents and school personnel are deeply and permanently embedded in their relationship and in the school context. These tensions become apparent only when there is conflict between the two groups or some sort of oppositional behavior by the parents. The greatest level of conflict occurs when low-income bicultural parents become so dissatisfied with their children's schools that they take collective action to correct them.[3] This type of behavior is highly problematic for school personnel however in that it contradicts their expectation of having a compliant bicultural parent population which follows the dictates of the school without question.

In this chapter I will focus on three specific areas of tension that exist in the relationship between bicultural parents and the schools: these areas are culture, knowledge, and power. I chose these three areas because in my experience in working with bicultural parents these have provided the greatest areas of tension, primarily because they are the most apparent and most "tangible" and are manifested on a daily basis in the relationship between bicultural parents and school personnel. What is more, the inability of current parent involvement practices to take into account the issue of contradictions in knowledge, culture, and power in regard to bicultural parents has contributed greatly to the alienation of these communities from the education process.

Tensions in Culture

Núñez[4] employs the concept of the briefcase, or the *maleta*, to illustrate how the U.S. education system devalues the native culture of Latino children. He argues that these children arrive to school on the first day with an imaginary *maleta*. This *maleta* contains the child's life knowledge; knowledge obtained during a five-plus year relationship with his/her family and culture: i.e., language, values, customs, traditions, worldview, etc. This *maleta* represents everything the child is familiar with and holds dear. Upon arriving at school, however, the teacher orders the bicultural child to empty his/her *maleta* because those possessions have no place or value in the classroom.

This is done both explicitly and implicitly through teaching practices and expectations that focus on "transitioning" or "assimilating" the bicultural child into the "mainstream." Teachers make it clear to bicultural students that they will be given "new" and "better" things to fill their *maletas* with. For English Learners this has been demonstrated in the longstanding educational practice of eradicating their native tongue and culture. Meanwhile the English-speaking white child is allowed to bring his/her briefcase into the classroom with all of his/her belongings intact because English will be spoken and promoted as the superior language, the curriculum will reflect his/her background and culture, and "white cultural values" will form the basis of the relationship between the teacher and the students.

Accordingly, just as bicultural children arrive at the United States' schools with their *maletas*, so do their parents. Latino, African-American, low-income, and immigrant parents also bring with them cultural capital and cultural perspectives which mediate how they interact and respond to their social and economic surroundings, including the school system.[5] And, as their children often do, bicultural parents frequently find the American schooling process completely alien, particularly since they are expected to follow and mimic the parenting strategies of middle- and upper-class white parents.

Tensions in Immigrant Parents' School Involvement

Immigrant parents must come to terms early on in their children's educational experience that their physical presence is expected at the school, lest they be considered uncaring parents. Indeed, in my discussions with immigrant Latino parents in San Diego I found that many of whom I have worked with have come to the realization that in America's schools you must actively protect and advocate for your child's educational rights. As read in the following words of a Latina parent advocate from San Diego, a parent who invests time in their children's education reaps the greatest rewards for them.

I've been here in the United States a very short time and I'm very interested in my children's educational opportunities. I understand that parents here need to be very involved, 100% if possible, in the schools in order to obtain greater opportunities for our children.

Immigrant parents also realize very quickly that the school system in the United States functions much differently than in their countries of origin, often presenting a contradiction with their personal experience of how schools functioned in their native countries. Ramirez, for example, documents the voices of a group of immigrant Latino parents who despite making concerted efforts to be active participants in their children's education still felt "unaware of the many traditions of school life" in the United States. One of the "traditions" he mentions is "parent involvement" and how this concept contradicts the parents' beliefs who "felt it was not their place to attend or to go to the schools for they felt the teachers were better suited to teach and educate their children."[6]

The concept of actively advocating for their children's education is often a new concept for many immigrant parents who came from countries in which this practice is not the norm, and they often believe that the burden of the responsibility for educating children should be on the school. In the United States, however, parent involvement is not only "accepted" (provided it doesn't include scrutiny of the school or its personnel) but expected if children are to succeed. This concept creates a personal contradiction for many immigrant parents who trust the school and value the responsibility of the teacher and the education system. The notion that a parent must be actively involved in educational matters in order to oversee that the school is doing its job and to assure that all children are receiving a good education presents a major inconsistency for many immigrant parents who believe that the schools should assume their responsibility and educate every child equitably. Moreover, this contradiction is further complicated when the schools exclusively blame the parents for their children's educational difficulties.

As a result of the contradictions between what the immigrant parents know about schools through their lived experiences and what the U.S. school system expects from them, these parents are often unable to deal with an educational system in which direct and visible parental participation is not only expected but demanded for student success. And for immigrant parents who fail to partake in this expected American behavior, their inaction is very often interpreted by school personnel as indifference, disinterest, or incompetence. This is perhaps the most dumbfounding of contradictions for immigrant parents who view teachers and educators as the people who know best for their children yet are the very people that push them away from the school when they have questions or concerns. One parent I used to work with in San Diego summed this paradox for immigrant parents as one of being invited to the school as a guest only to have the chair pulled out from under them when they try to get comfortable.

Bicultural Home Support

Regardless of the school's perception, "bicultural children operate competently in the home prior to entering the school system."[7] The home of the bicultural child is a rich social and cultural context for learning and cognition, even if it "differs" from that of the dominant culture in America. In fact, in spite of commonly accepted and frequently unchallenged deficit views of the bicultural family, the literature suggests that even in the "poorest" of homes, literacy and learning activities are present.

Despite this body of literature, however, bicultural communities are still often viewed by school personnel as being deficient. Teachers and administrators often hold the belief that the inability of bicultural students to succeed in a "meritocratic" institution such as public education is not representative of the inequities found in the educational process but in the inability of the linguistically or culturally diverse group to assimilate into, and take advantage of, the dominant culture's institutions. Specifically, it represents the bicultural parents' inability to work the system for their children. Dunn, for example, claimed that Latino parents have not held up their part of the responsibility for educating their children. He held the belief that "teachers are not miracle workers" and that "Hispanic pupils and their parents have also failed the schools and society, because they have not been motivated and dedicated enough to make the system work for them."[8] Thus, the point of view held by Dunn (and by many others) brings forth the conclusion that the failure of bicultural communities to measure up to Anglo-American perceptions of success is reflective of inherent cultural inadequacies or deficiencies that limit their ability to succeed in American schools and in society.

For those students who come from lower socioeconomic or bicultural families, sure, there is an obvious disadvantage in achieving the goal of academic success; but not because their cultural capital is not of worth, but rather because the school system devalues what they bring to the school. Cultural resistance on the part of the dominant cultural group has left the bicultural family alienated from mainstream educational institutions. This bias comes as a result of the Euro-centric partiality found in our public schools and the embedded racism that drives the relationship between school personnel and parents of color. To be sure, the public education system is firmly rooted and grounded in the white culture and has as its primary purpose to prepare middle- and upper-class white children to participate in their own culture. As a result, bicultural parents who do not possess this cultural capital find it difficult to navigate the schooling system and are resisted when they attempt to do so beyond the expected limits.

One final caveat, however, before we continue to the next section. Discussing culture within a context of understanding the relationship between bicultural parents and the public school system is an extremely difficult task. Most bodies of work tend to present culture as a concrete, monolithic, or materialistic characteristic of a certain group of people, while others tend to over-generalize modes of expression and negotiation to the entire cultural group in question. Consequently, there is a tendency to provide educators with "strategies" and "methods" for working with bicultural parent groups. Culture, however, is dynamic and fluid and has many intersects, the most notable of which are class and power.[9] These intersects provide challenges for educators in that they must question how these are manifested in their relationships with people who do not possess the cultural capital that the school values.

While there is a perceived need on the part of the school system to align the home culture to that of the school, the apparent need lies in understanding how school personnel, explicitly and implicitly, devalue the home culture of bicultural communities and to understand the attitudes and expectations of teachers and administrators who interact with low-income bicultural parents on a daily basis. Indeed, what I have laid out thus far points to understanding how deficit thinking, entrenched in the social practices of our country, functions to deflect scrutiny from embedded social and institutional contradictions by blaming the subordinate cultures.

Tensions in Knowledge

The type of knowledge we possess and the value placed on that knowledge vary among individuals and social groups. Knowing how to read, how to ride a bike, how to drive a manual transmission car, how to milk a cow, etc. are all distinct types of knowledge which are valued differently according to the context. For example, if I lived in a rural farming community, "farm related" knowledge would probably be more useful than a Ph.D. in education. Likewise, if I lived in a big urban metropolis, which I do, knowing how to ride the subway and hail a taxi would be useful knowledge, more so than knowing how to ride a horse, for example. In other words, the knowledge we possess varies in value and utility depending on the context.

Another distinction that is often made in human knowledge is how one "acquired" it. That is, does your knowledge of the literature of Carlos Fuentes come from your own personal readings of his work and your personal interpretations, or does this knowledge come from an advanced degree in Latin American literature in which respected university professors told you what the literacy experts had to say about his work? Does it matter? For many people in the United States, particularly educators, it does.

Knowledge in the United States is a commodity. And according to this logic, knowledge is quantifiable and measurable. The more you "have" the better you are. It can be measured by how many books you've read, by how many diplomas and certificates you have on your wall, and by how well you've done on standardized tests (such as IQ tests, college entrance exams, etc.). This is the only type of knowledge that is really universally valued in the United States, knowledge which is bought and paid for and which leads to some sort of certification or degree. As a result, the argument goes, if a parent does not have a formal education by studying at prestigious institutions of higher education then she/he must defer the decisions to their intellectual superiors who do, namely the teachers and the administration.

In the K-12 public schools, teachers and administrators reflect this quantified knowledge. They, through their formal education and formal training are representative of the highly valued book knowledge that is essential for academic success and social enlightenment in this country. They posses the skills necessary to do a particular job, in this case "educate" children (and when need be, their parents) on what they need to know to be successful in this country. They put the information out there for the students and their parents and those who work diligently to "pick it up" are rewarded via good grades and positive interactions with the teachers and the administration. And for those who enter the school system with "no knowledge," they are "filled up" with that which school personnel feel they are lacking.

This view of teachers and school administrators as the sole possessors and disseminators of knowledge is highly problematic, however, in that it reinforces the hegemonic status and power of the school personnel as well as the belief that parents who lack formal education are incapable of participating in decisions they have not been "trained in." There is also an oppressive premise to a schooling process which views formal education as superior to traditional forms of knowledge, particularly when school personnel themselves end up believing this is so, which is often the case. School personnel who view themselves as exclusively owning the rights to knowledge also participate in actively *devaluing* the life knowledge of working-class, bicultural, and immigrant parents and their children, and this creates tension. They tend to view bicultural parents as not being their intellectual equals, thus incapable of becoming authentic education partners. These are the educators that speak of the *need* to "educate" bicultural parents and of inviting them to workshops where they can pick up "parenting tips" to improve their home condition and their children's life chances.

When school personnel tend to hold the view that the knowledge bicultural parents possess is inferior or non-existent in comparison to theirs or more affluent parents, the problem of academic underachievement of bicultural students is situated in the families' and the communities' "deficiencies." In turn, parent involvement policies in schools that deal with large groups of linguistically and ethnically diverse parents take on a paternalistic quality whereby the effort is placed on changing or "educating" the parents instead of reforming the inequalities and inequities found in the school.[10] This naturally also creates tension, particularly when the parents perceive they are being treated as "dummies."

Paulo Freire once wrote that "no one knows it all; no one is ignorant of everything."[11] What he was suggesting is that we are all somewhere in that middle ground. We all possess some knowledge or skill that others may not, yet that does not make us smarter or better than others. Furthermore we all can learn new things. Within the school context, unfortunately, this often is not the case. Freire's classic critique of the *banking model*[12] of education still rings true in many cases in that many educators still consider themselves the owners and purveyors of knowledge and their students, and often their parents, as empty shells, and this is noticeably reflected in their relationship with them.

This quantification of knowledge has also been known to lead to self-deprivation on the part of bicultural parents and communities whereby they too begin to view their knowledge as inferior in comparison to the dominant population. Hence, at times bicultural parents begin to exclusively place the blame for academic underachievement on themselves or their children. They feel that because they themselves did not have the opportunity to further their own formal education that they are somehow lacking in their abilities to contribute to their children's education and to the school's policies. As a result, they are embarrassed to show up at the schools or humbly accept the opinions of the "experts" as true, even if these opinions are critiques aimed at them and their community.

As a final note to this section, I would like to briefly bring up one of the clearest contradictions inherent in knowledge as a form of social and cultural capital. It comes from the work of Foucault[13] who argued, in a general sense, that knowledge could not be separated from power or those groups in power; specifically the fact that those who define what legitimate knowledge or "truth" is are those who possess the power to enforce it as such. In other words, those with the most power in any society are also those whose ideas are considered to be universal and unbiased truths. Thus, we must ask ourselves if the inherent tensions and contradiction that I point out relate to issues of knowledge, or do they relate more closely to the issue of power? I will bring up this subject for the remainder of this chapter.

Tensions in Power Relations

Bicultural parents often enter the school system with a wide-eyed innocence; initially faithful to a system they believe will help their children surpass their own social status. They bring with them hope and trust and the belief that the schools will work exclusively to serve their children's interest. Yet, they become discouraged and even mistrustful when they attempt to advocate for their children and realize that they have entered a "contested public sphere . . . with neither resources nor power."[14] Indeed, low-income bicultural parents quickly become attuned to their low power status when they are caught in a process of actively advocating for their children's educational rights only to be neutralized and dismissed by school personnel.

The power I will speak of in the following sections can be classified into three certain areas: economic power, cultural power, and political power. Lareau and Horvat[15] identify similar concepts of power in terms of capital: social capital, or "social relations to promote advancement"; cultural capital, which is "cultural knowledge or resources"; and economic capital, which is "economic resources."

Economic Power

Economic power is at the root of all status and social powers in our country. Those who have greater access to wealth and wealth production are afforded rights and privileges that are for the most part out of reach for the "common" citizen. Economic power in our country provides a greater sense of independence and leverage for those who possess it, most obviously due to the fact that the majority of things in our country are quantified and given a monetary value. In our country price is equivalent to quality. The more you pay for something, the better the assumed quality. This goes for both tangibles (most notably material items) and non-tangibles (such as private education, legal counsel, health care, etc.).

Economic power also has obvious advantages for a parent whose child is struggling in school. The most significant advantage is that of the resources at their disposal. High-income parents have several options at hand that can significantly improve their children's learning outcomes and life chances. The supplemental learning experiences high-income parents can provide for their children can come in the form of trips (both out-of-state and out-of-country, or to local areas of interest), learning materials (such as books, computers, etc.), or remedial services and one-on-one tutoring.

Economic power is also quite important for parents who are having difficulty with the school in that it significantly improves their chances of effectively advocating for their children when the school personnel are unreceptive. High-income parents can hire their own psychologist when their child has been denied entry into a gifted student program or can search for a "second opinion" when their child is to be placed in Special Education. Most importantly, however, high-income parents can hire legal representation when the school fails to fulfill its duty.

Legal representation, and the high price of having it, is a major obstacle for low-income and working-class people in our society. Often when low-income parents are in need of legally challenging their children's school or school district, they find themselves turning to the state departments of education, the state boards, or local community advocacy groups for help. Seldom do these actions reap significant outcomes, however, because more often than not state agencies are slow, bureaucratic, and reflective of the dominant ideologies and interests, thus of very little use; and local and state advocacy groups and lawyers are often over-worked and focused on more high-profile issues than low-income parents looking to remedy child- and school-specific issues.

In our society there are clearly asymmetrical economic power relations between the dominant group and the subordinate groups, the latter who are of course primarily bicultural. This asymmetry in economic power (or capital) limits the options bicultural communities have at their disposal to claim what they are entitled to, in this case access to a quality education. Moreover, economic power is inseparable from status and cultural power. This is perhaps one of the greatest advantages high-income parents have as a result of having economic power: status and privilege.

Cultural Power

Just as important, or perhaps even more important, than having economic power in our country is having status and cultural power.

These "non-tangible" forms of capital figure significantly in how individuals and social groups are allotted rights and privileges in our society and its institutions, particularly education.

The concept of cultural capital is significant in our analysis of status power for low-income bicultural parents. Cultural capital, in a general sense, refers to the "general cultural background, knowledge, disposition, and skills that are passed on from one generation to another.[16] In our discussion of bicultural parents' relationship with the schools, it brings us back to the concept of the *maleta* and what a child and parent bring to the classroom and the school for cultural capital represents the "cultural knowledge and resources" from which bicultural families draw upon to make sense of and survive in their world. This form of capital, while powerful for them, is not necessarily equally valued at school, however. Rather, the cultural power and resources that bicultural students and parents bring to the school context are actually at odds with the dominant cultural capital.

From this perspective, the school system's ability to de-legitimize and devalue bicultural capital is closely linked to issues of power and the creation of dominant and subordinate cultures.[17] The power relations found in this relationship thus forces us to expand our view of culture to include issues of class formation and class relations. In other words, "social class position and class culture become a form of cultural capital in the school setting."[18] Therefore, the complexity of understanding displays of cultural capital by bicultural parents is complicated by school personnel's low expectations and low desires to work with bicultural parents who are also of low social standing.

Most interactions between school personnel and subordinate parent populations closely resemble what Freire calls cultural invasion. Freire describes the process of cultural invasion as when "the invaders penetrate the cultural context of another group, in disrespect of the latter's potentialities; they impose their own view of the world upon those they invade."[19] Along this line of reasoning, in the school context we see that while in theory the primary function of schools is to serve the interest of the community and its student population, in reality the schools have historically functioned to serve outside interests. Watts likens the role of the school to that of a "colonial model that serves an external authority,"[20] one that imposes the values, desires, and world view of the dominant group onto the subordinate populations, or those with less political power, even in neighbor-hoods where the "minority" population is the "majority."

Status and Political Power

High-paying, professional white-collar jobs and wealth bestow "hegemonic status"[21] on individuals and groups in our society for it is understood that the wealthy have earned their right to dominate. It is assumed that a wealthy person is more intelligent, hardworking, and ambitious than a person who is employed in a low-paying, manual labor job, thus worthy of more respect.

Having status is best reflected in the treatment rich parents re-ceive when they interact with school personnel. They are welcomed and treated as wanted guests (at least in their presence), and they are frequently consulted on issues that affect their children and the school. Moreover, their children are allotted high quality educational opportunities that will prepare them to follow in their parents' foot-steps. The essential contradiction within the school system, and the resulting tension, is that the school system should ideally work to serve the interests of *all* children and their communities. Parents, whether rich or poor, should be treated respectfully and their interac-tions with the school should be authentic. Yet, the truth is that the low social status of bicultural parents places them in a position of constant struggle with the school system.

In our society, a lack of political power is inseparably tied to a lack of economic and status power. This lack of political power is most evident in our neglected low-income bicultural communities in which politicians and school officials are only seen during campaign stops or photo opportunities. This lack of political power became apparent to me during my teaching career in San Diego when a group of parents I worked with, all low-income, Spanish-speaking, immi-grant parents, were making repeated attempts to speak to a school board member about problems at their children's school but were always summarily denied until a more powerful political figure in the Latino community made the request on their behalf.

Political power is most obviously tied to economic power, yet it is also closely tied to social relations (e.g., social capital). High income parents often have great political power in their communities as well as many friends and acquaintances at their disposal to have their voices heard. This "connectedness" is often characterized as the power of "who you know." Indeed, having strong political allies in our country automatically warrants you greater attention and a higher level of responsiveness by those in power.

Many of the immigrant Latino parents I have worked with have been most affected by this lack of social capital. Not so much in terms of not having strong social relationships, these they have, but in terms of not having access to people in power. In the many years I have worked with bicultural parents in Southern California, I have seen many of them make numerous attempts to step forward and become active members of the education community. Yet, according to them and my own personal observations, their attempts have often been rebuffed by an educational bureaucracy full of tensions and contradictions, a system that promotes an illusion of inclusion but in reality presents a gated community for those already in power.

The feelings of political powerlessness and frustration felt by the Latino parents I worked with were also being felt by many other parents from the district I worked in at the time, and these were articulated in a 2002 opinion editorial article in the local daily paper by a leading San Diego parent advocate who wrote:

> For the last four years, I've watched month in and month out at school board meetings while parents, grandparents, teachers, district employees, and students came before this board and pleaded their cause. And month in and month out, I've watched the frustration on too many people's faces as the minute buzzer rang, signaling the end to any hopes or dreams they may have entertained that their words would matter. The pro-[superintendent] board president then simply called, "Next," and another deluded American tiptoed to the microphone—hoping against hope his/her words might make a difference to a board elected to represent her/his needs. The only testimony this board has gone out of its way to acknowledge and encourage has been that of those who agreed with them . . .—people with power and money. For these people, the board president turned off the timer and let them say whatever they wanted—for as long as they wanted.[22]

This is an articulate testimony, not so much for its demonstration of the parents' lack of voice in so-called democratic participation but rather in its portrayal in the *denial* of their voice. Bicultural parents make many attempts to interact effectively with the school system yet they often find that navigating through an intensely political and bureaucratic institution which is unwilling to authentically collaborate with them is a much greater challenge than they had envisioned or expected.

Participating in the school bureaucracy beyond superficial levels is what makes the contradictions more obvious to those low-income bicultural parents who wish to navigate the system this far. The more a bicultural parent attempts to get involved in the school system, the more they become aware of the false promises and the disingenuous relationship they have with school bureaucrats. It is through these lived experiences that bicultural parents come to the realization that their input is neither warranted nor valued. Upon this realization, the parents take various paths. Either they get discouraged to the point that they no longer wish to participate, due to the fact that they've unmasked the hypocrisy of the school system, or they develop an oppositional and mistrustful attitude, and in the end participate in challenging the dominant power structure.

Coercive and Collaborative Power Relations

Cummins contends that in analyzing the variables that contribute to bicultural student failure and bicultural community exclusion, "it becomes evident that power and status relations between dominant and subordinate groups exert a major influence."[23] He argues that since schools participate in a very real power struggle between themselves and the parents, true partnership between the two is precluded by "coercive" power relations. These coercive power relations are played out through interpersonal relationships that place low-income, bicultural parents in subordinate positions, denying them a voice in decisions that affect their children's education.

The argument that bicultural parents are often ignored as legitimate stakeholders in their children's education or coerced by school personnel into buying into policies and practices which they were neither consulted about nor asked to participate in, is frequently due to the fact that they often hold little economic, political, and social capital power. The low-status that bicultural parents occupy in society is clearly reflected in the school system when they try to demand what their children are entitled to yet are effectively systematically shunned and rebuffed by school personnel.

It is in these instances of unsuccessful advocacy that bicultural parents begin to experience their lack of power and the coercive power relations Cummins speaks of. As a consequence, when it comes to school policy, bicultural parents usually have decisions imposed on them and their children. They are not consulted when there are educational decisions to be made nor are they even informed. White, middle- and upper- class parents, however, influence as well as participate in decision-making processes at their children's school. In fact, schools actively seek out their input and participation, particularly when it is financial in nature.

Figure 2 demonstrates how I see the flow of power and input in bicultural community schools in comparison to schools which have a predominantly white, middle- and upper-class student and parent population.

Figure 2: Dominant Culture Parents vs. Bicultural Parents in School/ Community Power Relations

In this figure, we see that parents from the dominant culture are active participants in the decision-making process in the school and are allowed to provide input due to their social, political, and financial capital and the school personnel's perception that these parents are their social equals. On the other hand, students and parents from bicultural communities have policies imposed on them by those in power, namely school personnel and policymakers, thereby ignoring any accountability that the school may have to the community. In other words, the "schools systematically exclude low-income parents and communities from participating in school management and oversight, and through this exclusion severely limit the ability of these actors to hold schools accountable for educational failure."[24]

In regard to the coercive power exerted by school personnel, Cummins suggests that it is "important to note that students (and communities) do not passively accept" their impositions. To the contrary, subordinate groups often "resist this process of subordination actively through disruptive or oppositional behavior."[25] These demonstrations of "home power" demonstrate that while bicultural parents are limited in their expressions of power, they are not powerless. To the contrary, bicultural parents, students, and communities have long demonstrated their home power through walk-outs, protests, and legal challenges against the school system. Often, however, the reaction by the school system has been to constrain and squelch such resistance, often quite effectively, rather than attempt to understand the root causes of such behavior.

Understanding School Tensions

The inability of current parent involvement policy and practice to take into account contradictions and tensions in knowledge, culture, and power, particularly in regard to bicultural parents, has contributed greatly to the alienation of these communities from the schooling process. Apparently it is much easier for school personnel to see the problem of bicultural parent involvement within the particular group than within the school culture and their micro-interactions with them. To conclude this chapter, I will summarize the tensions that were discussed thus far.

In a general sense, the argument I am making is that the school system is rife with contradictions, contradictions which embed tensions between itself and bicultural communities. These tensions are rooted in the contradictory nature of the schooling process which promotes itself as a neutral and value free institution but which implicitly recreates the asymmetrical power structure and inequities of our society. This could best be understood by examining school ideologies in regard to culture, knowledge, and power, as I suggest. These three constructs, in my opinion, provide us with concrete examples of contradictions that exist within the school system that preclude an authentic partnership with bicultural and low-income parents.

I specifically argue that the school system only values "formal" means of knowledge acquisition. School personnel tend to view those individuals who have gone to college and have received a degree as smart or capable. Low-income, bicultural parents, on the other hand, come to school with "home knowledge," knowledge that they've acquired through lived experiences and the hardships of being of low-income. This knowledge is not recognized as a legitimate form of knowledge in the schools, however, so school personnel are quick to dismiss these parents as incapable of making decisions that will affect their children's academic endeavors. This contradictory view of what constitutes knowledge creates an embedded, dialectical tension that makes it difficult for school personnel to accept the bicultural parents' input. By the same token, bicultural parents also sense this climate of devaluing home knowledge and therefore are often hesitant to contribute their opinions.

I also pointed out that there are tensions in culture present because the school system "reflects only the experiences and values of middle- [and upper]-class English-speaking students and effectively suppresses the experiences and values of culturally diverse students."[26] This orientation toward the white middle- and upper-class thus negates the cultural capital that bicultural parents and students bring to the school. As a result, schools feel the need to find ways to compensate for the presumed cultural deficiencies, such as language, customs, values, etc. This is best reflected in the struggles bicultural parents face as they attempt to secure bilingual instruction for their children. These contradictions and tensions are also present in the relationship between school personnel and African-Americans, Native Americans, Indochinese, and other immigrant groups who struggle to retain some form of identity and input into their children's formal education process.

And finally, the contradictions and tensions embedded in the power struggles between bicultural parents and the school system can best be analyzed by examining their interpersonal relationships. Often the school system takes a coercive power stance against bicultural communities with the understanding that these parents have "power constraints." This is often demonstrated in the school system's imposition of policies and practices that deny bicultural parents a legitimate voice in the education of their children. The tension here, however, develops when subordinate communities challenge the schools' power structure and make attempts to be heard.

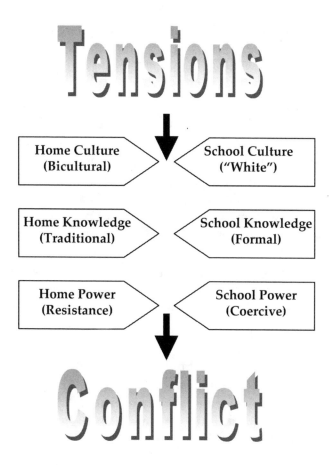

Figure 3: Tensions in Culture, Knowledge, and Power in the Public Schools

The tensions outlined in this chapter are ever present and embedded in the relationship between bicultural communities and the public school system, as can be seen in Figure 3. Most times these tensions go unnoticed or are able to be neutralized or deflected by the dominant institution, particularly when they are brought to the fore by a small, yet critical, number of individuals. The larger movements of dissatisfaction against the schooling system often occur when the contradictions reach extreme levels of tension. These conflicts could be the result of bicultural parents who question the racist practices of schooling or bicultural parents' struggles to be heard by school personnel.

In the next chapter we will look at how bicultural parents resist the workings of the school system when they begin to unmask the contradictions inherent in the school system and actively work to take up their own struggles for educational justice and equity.

Critical Incident

Kimberley Elementary is a large urban school in Southern California comprised primarily of low-income, Latino parents who work in the nearby downtown hotels and restaurants. Parent involvement at Kimberley Elementary is primarily limited to parents attending fieldtrips with their children or attending *Back to School Night* and other social events. For the most part, school personnel and teachers appear to get along at the school and they both appear to be happy and cordial.

Mrs. Hernandez, a parent of two students, has been active at Kimberley Elementary for the last four years. While initially Mrs. Hernandez began her involvement by volunteering in her son's classroom checking off homework and making copies for the teacher, currently she finds herself on the school's governance team, the School Site Council, and the English Learner Advisory Committee. Despite sitting on these important committees, however, Mrs. Hernandez is unsatisfied with her role as parent representative. Several things have taken place during her time at the school that makes her wonder if her input is authentic or even valued.

First, Mrs. Hernandez is concerned that she was never elected by the other parents to participate on these committees; rather the administrator "invited" her to participate. And, every year when she asks if there should be an official election for these posts, the administrator or the school secretary always tells her that "the other parents don't want to participate on these committees" or "the other parents are not as aware of what is going on at the school" as she is, so she is the best person for the job.

Another issue that has Ms. Hernandez believing that she is not an authentic representative for the parents is that she does not receive the agendas for the upcoming meetings in time nor is she invited to staff meetings or district trainings that will help her understand the issues being brought forth at these meetings. Rather, the process has been that either the teachers on the committees or the administrator give her the "gist" of the issues being discussed and ask her to sign where a parent representative signature is needed.

Finally, Mrs. Hernandez is also concerned with the fact that: there is no forum for her to share what she is voting on with the other parents to get their feedback; she is still unfamiliar with the protocols of the meetings and how items are placed on the agendas; and lastly, most of the information presented to her is in English, which is her second language, and in highly technical terms. In short, Mrs. Hernandez wonders if she is being manipulated by the school personnel and is considering resigning.

Questions for Reflection

1. Are Mrs. Hernandez's concerns about the situation at her children's school warranted?
2. Should Mrs. Hernandez resign from her committee posts to stand up for her values?
3. What other steps can Mrs. Hernandez take to demonstrate her concerns?
4. Are there some embedded tensions in the relationship between Mrs. Hernandez and the school personnel? If so, what are they? Culture? Knowledge? Power?
5. What kind of power relations do we see in the relationship between Mrs. Hernandez and the school personnel?
6. What can school personnel do to address Mrs. Hernandez's concerns?

Disinterest or Resistance?

Popular belief within the U.S. public education system is that bicultural parents neither participate nor want to participate in the schooling process of their children, and their absence has often been viewed as indifference or incompetence. The low turnout of bicultural parents at school meetings and school-sponsored events brings out a barrage of complaints from teachers, administrators, and policymakers who continually ask questions such as: Why won't these parents participate? Don't these parents value their children's education? What can we do to get these parents more involved?

Missing from this line of questioning is an analysis of the quality of involvement that is being asked of low-income bicultural parents and the treatment they receive when they *do* become involved or when they overstep their expected roles. Most parent involvement policies, for example, are embedded in the notion that the function of the parents is to blindly support the schools' and the teachers' efforts to educate the students without question. In more affluent communities this support often takes on the form of fundraising. Parents are urged to donate money to purchase new playground equipment, computers, and supplementary textbooks. In schools located in low-income communities, where the parents do not have the resources to support the school in such endeavors, the expected involvement is quite different, however.

Parent involvement for bicultural parents usually consists of activities that will keep them busy and contained: making copies, cutting paper, or babysitting other parents' children who are attending parenting classes. Efforts by educators to keep bicultural parents occupied while keeping them at bay have precluded the development of a meaningful partnership based on mutual respect and responsibility. In addition, these practices have created distrust and indifference on the part of bicultural parents, particularly for those who have become cognizant of the contradictions in the school system's messages and the fact that their input and participation, while sought, is not authentically valued.

In the previous chapters we analyzed the relationship between school personnel and low-income bicultural parents from the point of view of the school and society. Using a structural exploitation and race relations lens I laid out how I believe school personnel, both consciously and unconsciously, negatively interact with and treat low-income bicultural parents. Additionally, we also looked at the embedded tensions caused by contradictory notions of knowledge, culture, and power. Now the task at hand is to look at and analyze how bicultural parents relate to and respond to the school personnel given the current situation of inauthentic participation. More specifically, we need to look at how bicultural parents respond to oppressive parent involvement policies and practices.

Notwithstanding the structural exploitation and race relation arguments made thus far to explain why bicultural parents are excluded from authentically participating in the school system, certain key questions still remain for understanding this relationship. Specifically, given the somewhat gloomy insight I have provided into the relationship between bicultural parents and the schools thus far, we must pose the following questions to clarify this issue: Don't bicultural parents have *any* say in what goes on at their children's schools? That is, isn't there some sort of free will or human agency on the part of bicultural parents involved in the previously presented scenarios? Don't bicultural parents also have to do their part to assure their children's success in school and in future endeavors?

Certainly, low-income bicultural parents *do* have and make choices, they are not objects. They *do* possess agency, and as all humans, the ability to act upon their world. To this, I agree. Thus, when considering the problem of why more bicultural parents do not get involved at their children's schools at the levels we would like, we must not only look at what limits their participation and what is expected of them when they do show up, but we must also consider how they act and react to the schools' insincere overtures. That is, we have looked at how the school acts upon bicultural parents, now our task is to look at how bicultural parents act upon the school.

I propose the following perspective when considering the issue of why low-income bicultural parents do not participate in large numbers at their children's schools, even on those days when they do "have the time." I argue that the absence of bicultural parents in the schools is more a demonstration of resistance (a defense mechanism against oppression and humiliation) than a sign of disinterest, even though it is often viewed as the latter.

Resistance

In previous chapters I laid out the argument that the public school system is for the most part a biased and domineering institution. It imposes a worldview onto bicultural students and their parents that perpetuates an existing social structure of inequality. This is possible via asymmetrical power relations which put bicultural parents in a subordinate position and deficit (racist) thinking which views people of color as deficient and lacking.

Yet, there is a certain "incompleteness" to domination. That is, no domination is complete; rather, domination is imperfect and always highly contested. Consequently, domination must not be seen as absolute or as functioning unchallenged but as a struggle between the dominant culture and subordinate groups in multiple institutions and settings. Lareau and Horvat, for example, put forward that "reproduction is jagged and uneven and is continually negotiated by social actors."[1] A similar position is posed by Darder who writes, "Whether hegemony takes place in school, the mass media, or other social institutions, it must constantly be fought for to be maintained." Darder continues by stating that this is often due to the "changing nature of historical circumstances and the complex demands and critical actions of human beings."[2] Thus, in order to clearly understand this notion of resistance, we must understand domination as a partial and dialectical process.

Posited within Marx's notion "that history unfolds dialectically," Persell writes about the complexity of maintaining a *structure of dominance* in society:

> Since complex totalities are comprised of a number of elements and tendencies, these processes may change at different speeds or in incompatible ways, leading to contradictions within the system and ultimately, perhaps, to the transformation of the system. The notion of contradiction suggests that education does not merely reproduce the social relations of production in an orderly fashion, but also contains potential for change.[3]

The contradictions which are inherent within the societal *structure of dominance*, thus within the institution of schooling, are sources of constant tension between the dominant and subordinate cultures. In the broader society, these tensions arise from the contradictions related to economic interests, class divisions, ideological differences, and race relations. In the school setting, I maintain the contradictions are often found in issues related to knowledge, culture, and power.

To be sure, we find some profound social contradictions in our country, which is touted as the most advanced in the history of the world. We find an ever-increasing number of people living in poverty and despair; we fill our prisons at significantly higher rates than most other developed nations, mostly with Blacks and Latinos; we find the national distribution of wealth going increasingly and shamelessly from the poor and middle income sectors of society to the upper economic segments of the nation; and we find the poor and working-class fighting wars which most benefit the rich and privileged. This list can obviously go on, but for now let's just say that there is a constant overarching contradiction in the United States' inability to match its rhetoric with its policies and practices. This in turn causes tensions at various levels of society as various groups and individuals struggle to interpret and challenge them while at the same time the dominant group works to maintain them. Therefore, contradictions are also found in the public school system and in the education process.

Quite possibly one of the most critical of the contradictions in our nation's public school system is its inability to close the educational achievement disparity between specific social groups and middle- and upper-class white students. This is problematic to many educators and education advocates alike because the public education system promotes itself as a value-free, unbiased institution where every student will be allotted an equal opportunity to succeed and will be judged on their individual merit. Yet, the consistent academic underachievement of low-income students of color and the treatment they and their parents receive within the schooling process bring these myths into question.

Notwithstanding this critique of the failings of the school system, I understand that free public education is a necessary institution in our country for it does provide advancement opportunities for a small number of low-income, bicultural students who may otherwise not have them. Thus another contradiction lies in the fact that despite the general ineffectiveness of the public school system in educating poor bicultural children, it still needs to be available to them, more so than for the affluent because this institution may be the only opportunity these students have to "prove" themselves and thus advance socially. It should come to no surprise then that it is the affluent sector of our society which often advocates doing away with public education using, ironically, the low-performance of low-income and bicultural students as proof of schools failing society.

For the most part these societal and institutional contradictions function unnoticed, obfuscated by hegemonic socialization practices inherent in our social system. Yet, these contradictions do not always go unobserved. Rather oftentimes these contradictions are exposed and sometimes conflict arises. I believe this happens in three instances:

1. When there is *symbolic dissonance*, that is, when the contradictions between rhetoric and practice reach such "extreme levels" that they become so apparent and impossible to ignore, particularly among the perceptions of the subordinate population;
2. When there is *personal dissonance*, as in when a person's lived experiences within the system unveil the contradictions. In other words, when what an individual or group is experiencing explicitly contradicts what they are being socialized to believe; and . . .
3. When there is *critical consciousness*, which means when members of the subordinate population become politically and critically conscious of their subordinate roles and begin to openly resist the hegemonic working of the dominant institutions, thus refusing to participate in their own oppression and domination.

The contradictions of the social system coupled with oppositional behaviors and ideologies by subordinate groups produce a less deterministic course of social reproduction than those outlined by traditional Marxist thought. For these reasons, the concepts of resistance, tension, and conflict figure significantly in any faithful analysis of the relationship between bicultural parents and the public school system, which can also be characterized as the relationship between subordinate groups and an institution of the dominant culture. Moreover, "models of resistance posit that domination is never as mechanistic as Social and Cultural Reproduction [sic] models would have us assume, and instead is highly contested in the dialectic between ideological and structural constraints and human agency."[4] Thus, within the public education system the dialectical nature of the relationship between the schools and bicultural students and their parents is therefore sometimes played out through submission and acceptance, and other times through resistance and even conflict.

The issue of resistance implies that there exist contested terrains within social institutions (in our case education) in which individuals or subordinate groups are able to resist and interrupt complete domination. The oppositional behavior members from subordinate groups exhibit has drawn the attention of educational theorists who attempt to understand how resistance functions in the relationship between the dominant and the subordinate cultures. Giroux, in particular, writes the following:

> Resistance is a valuable theoretical and ideological construct that provides an important focus for analyzing the relationship between school and the wider society. More importantly, it provides new theoretical leverage for understanding the complex ways in which subordinate groups experience educational failure.[5]

The schools system, however, often lacks opportunities for, and/or demonstrates a lack of interest in, understanding why and how resistance is manifested in bicultural groups and individuals. To the contrary, the response of the school system has often been to eliminate any type of resistance that disrupts the working of this institution. Often this is easy to carry out since the school system is a powerful institution that is able to dismiss and silence low-income bicultural individuals and groups who lack the status and the power to challenge it on equal footing.

Modes of Resistance

Understanding how and why certain individuals from subordinate groups choose to question, challenge, and resist places a significant amount of agency on individuals within social institutions. The form of resistance an individual chooses to use (whether consciously or subconsciously), however, is dependent upon a variety of factors: the situation, the person's lived experiences, the person's social status in regard to race, class, and gender, etc.

The way subordinate individuals interact with the contradictions they experience in institutional settings also run along several diverse continua. Cummins, for example, presents a continuum of how certain individuals may react to racism and discrimination in the school setting. These reactions range from an "internalization of a sense of ambivalence or insecurity" to the outright "rejection of, and active resistance to, dominant group values."[6] A caveat that Cummins presents to these two modes of resistance is that "at both extremes [of this continuum], the result has frequently been alienation from schooling and mental withdrawal from academic effort."[7]

In his analysis of the academic underachievement of bicultural students, Núñez paints a similar picture when he asserts that "many [bicultural] children react to the negative responses by teachers by rejecting the school code, disattending [sic] the school lessons, and replacing the school culture with a peer subculture from which they receive positive response."[8] Thus, the fact that individuals from subordinate groups will use a variety of means at their disposal to resist oppression and domination is complicated by the fact that "the solutions they often select arise from the ascribed beliefs and values of the dominant society, [thus], they may in fact [be leading] themselves and others deeper into forms of domination and oppression."[9]

Using the above scenarios, let's take a look at how resistance applies to parents. Bicultural parent resistance can also take on various forms, not all of which are easily discernable. The simplest and most common form of resistance comes in the form of absence, disengagement, or disinterest. In other words, many bicultural parents simply refuse to attend or participate in school-related activities that they believe are useless, particularly in light of other obligations they may have in regard to home or work. Indeed, what parent would want to attend and participate in school meetings in which the decisions have been made long before the parents were ever convened or sit for hours listening to a lecture by a teacher or administrator in a position of privilege scold them on how they should do more to help their children and the school?

Another form of resistance that is more observable and may occur among "more informed" bicultural parents is active oppositional behavior or openly challenging the school system. This oppositional behavior can take on distinct manifestations and is at times discouraging for bicultural parents who quickly come to the realization that their low power and social status standing makes it difficult for them to challenge the powerful institution of public education.

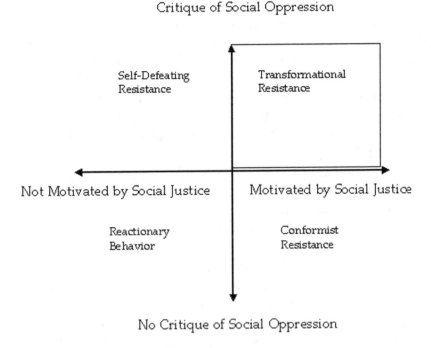

Figure 4: Defining the Concept of Resistance. Re-printed with permission © Corwin Press.

Solórzano and Delgado Bernal insightfully point out that while resistance has been the topic of many theoretical constructs which attempt to "demonstrate how individuals negotiate and struggle with structures and create meaning of their own from these interactions," most resistance theories have focused on "self-defeating" resistance in which the individuals' "behavior implicates them even further in their own domination."[10] To counteract this, Solórzano and Delgado Bernal present resistance as running along two axes which may or may not include a "critique of social oppression" and/or "an interest in social justice."

In Figure 4, we can see how these axes and their theoretical construct of resistance identify four types of resistance among bicultural students: *reactionary behavior, self-defeating resistance, conformist resistance,* and *transformational resistance.* Resistance as a topic of why bicultural parents actively, consciously or subconsciously, choose not to participate in the schools can be best analyzed using the typology suggested by Solórzano and Delgado Bernal.

The first mode of resistance identified is that of *reactionary behavior,* which the authors suggest is not resistance at all, but rather uncritical disruptive behavior. They identify this behavior as lacking "both a critique of her or his oppressive conditions and [a lack of motivation for] social justice."[11] In other words, the individual is just merely acting out for the "hell of it" or "to make the authority figure feel uncomfortable." In parents, this type of action is best seen in those who search for opportunities to be a thorn in the side of the administrators or teachers and who "nitpick" on issues of irrelevance. Often these behaviors may be the result of the parents' own negative schooling experiences or their distrust in the schooling system. Yet, what best describes these behaviors is that the actions are not driven by the individual's ability to name the context or social oppressive conditions that "contribute to her or his . . . behavior" nor are they motivated to improve the school or the situation, rather, they just "dislike" the principal or the teacher.

Self-defeating resistance is characterized as individuals who have "some critique of their oppressive social conditions but are not motivated by an interest in social justice." This type of resistance is that which has been heavily documented which analyzes how the actions of the "oppressed" contribute to their own subordination. The example most frequently cited is that of a drop-out student who "may have a compelling critique of the schooling system but then engages in behavior that is self-defeating and does not help transform her or his oppressive status."[12] Thus, this type of resistance is a form of escape from the oppressive condition but with no desire to transform it.

For bicultural parents, self-defeating resistance is best tied into their refusal to participate in school meetings that are either "boring" or "useless." These meetings represent oppressive conditions for they are characterized by domineering administrators who lecture parents rather than engage them. And while bicultural parents may indeed have legitimate reasons for not attending these school-sponsored events, their absence does little to change the conditions at the schools. To the contrary, it projects a perception of indifference and apathy, thus validating common preconceived deficit assumptions about bicultural parents. In light of this, I believe that low bicultural parent participation, while a form of resistance, is self-defeating in nature in that it not only lacks the critical political consciousness and organization necessary to demonstrate dissatisfaction with the unjust conditions at hand, but also lacks the foresight and the commitment to change or transform their root causes.

Solórzano and Delgado Bernal also identify *conforming resistance* as a type of oppositional behavior that challenges the dominant ideology yet falls along the line of the "liberal tradition" in which societal symptoms are handled by "Band-aid" solutions rather than from a focus on challenging the current system of oppression. Oftentimes, this conforming resistance is noticeable in how bicultural parents blame other bicultural parents for their lack of presence or individual responsibility at the school, as seen in the following words from a Latina parent in San Diego:

> If a parent truly wants to be involved, they'd even take the bus. I used to take two buses to get to my daughter's school or I would ask permission to go on the school bus with them. If a parent truly wants to be involved in their children's school, it doesn't matter if they're in Mexico, or Tijuana, or Los Angeles. You want to be involved and you're worried about your child's education, it doesn't matter where you are. You understand me? But, a parent who doesn't want to be involved will always find excuses.

For "more involved" bicultural parents this conformist resistance is sometimes demonstrated through parent/teacher organizations, English Learner Advisory Committees, or site governance committees which provide well structured and well regulated parental participation activities. Parent leaders on these committees frequently urge other parents to become more involved in groups such as these so that their "voices can be heard" yet fail to acknowledge their fundamental shallowness. And while important, rarely, if ever, do these types of committees actually "challenge institutional practices, question the relevancy of the pedagogy and curriculum, or examine the effects of socioeconomic factors."[13] Instead, these committees are merely there to provide lip-service and token parent involvement in advisory roles that hold no real or authentic power.

And finally, Solórzano and Delgado Bernal identify *transformational resistance* as a form of resistance which is motivated by social justice and has a critique of social oppression. In this mode of resistance there exists a "level of awareness and critique of . . . oppressive conditions and structures of domination and . . . a sense of social justice."[14] In this level of resistance the parents are not merely avoiding school meetings, satisfied with participating in low-impact roles, or exclusively blaming themselves and their fellow parents for their children's low-academic achievement. Instead, the parents are working to improve the condition of the entire school as well as working to name those elements of the schooling process which are detrimental to their children and not in the best interest of their community. In other words, they are able to recognize the elements of economic exploitation that negatively influence their community and identify those school practices which are racist and discriminatory against them and their children. More importantly, however, these parents act to change these practices and to transform them.

Resistance and Counter-Resistance

Bicultural parents are placed in a difficult situation when dealing with the schools. On the one hand, they are systematically excluded from authentically participating in the schools beyond menial tasks and then blamed when they are absent; furthermore, they are discouraged and resisted when they try to participate in more meaningful ways. Clearly bicultural parents have very well delineated roles in the school system. These roles require them to accept the authority of the school without question. However, such an "exclusionary orientation by the school can lead communities to challenge the institutional power structure."[15] That is, when low-income bicultural communities begin to uncover the contradictions that are inherent in the education system, they begin to resist and challenge that very system.

When low-income bicultural communities begin to resist the workings of the public education system, however, counter-resistance on the part of the institution often develops to diffuse and squelch their work. As a result, the parents' resistance is often short-lived or stifled. This is primarily due to the asymmetrical power relations which position the subordinate groups in the continual position of the underdog. In other words, the dominant institution has the power to employ means of counter-resistance, therefore de-legitimizing the subordinate populations' attempts to struggle for humanity and call attention to the contradictions. The most apparent reason for this is because school personnel know that these parents are limited in resources and often lack the technical knowledge of how to effectively challenge the system.

Through the voices of the many bicultural parents I have worked with, it has been acknowledged that there exists injustice, inequality, and inequity when it comes to the education of their children. However, in addition to educational policies and practices which negatively affect the academic success of their children, barriers are also present within the educational system that silence their voices when they make efforts to question these injustices. A barrier in this context is something that impedes a parent or community member from authentically participating in the school system. These barriers are neither exclusively placed within society, the school, the community, nor the individuals, but rather these barriers appear to be present in all four.

During my career as an educator and parent advocate I have come across many parent groups who have voiced concerns about the quality of their children's education, and I have helped them organize themselves to challenge the school system.[16] Their experiences with the school, however, point to barriers that have functioned as counter-resistance to their efforts to be more involved. For example, many bicultural parents I've worked with have expressed their concerns with the role of the school principal and how this individual often represents the most formidable barrier, or counter-resistance, to their efforts and struggles for educational justice for their children and their community.

Administrators as Counter-Resistance

Within the school setting the person with the most relative power is the principal. Countless bicultural parents I have come in contact with have indicated to me that these individuals are the persons that most impede their relationship with the school. Each one has a story to tell or supports the concept that the administrator at their site does not make any authentic attempt to work with bicultural parents or low-income communities. Instead, many bicultural parents, and teachers sympathetic to their work, often identify the school principal as a "dictator" who not only intimidates parents but students and teachers as well.

One parent from San Diego, for example, once told me about a situation that occurred at her school during the beginning of the 2002–2003 school year in which the administrator made it clear to the community (the majority low-income Latinos) that she did not want the parents involved:

> The principal didn't want the parents there. She directly said, "I don't want parents at the school." If the parents want to come, they will have to pass by a person who will guide them. [That person] will give [the parents] a specified hour, day, or time so that they can come at that time and they will have to pass a TB test, etc., etc.

When I asked this parent how the administrator at the site was able to promote a policy which explicitly excluded parents, she said that the principal did so in a "nice" manner, using "pretexts":

> We received a letter at the beginning of the week, during the first days of the school year, where it stated very nicely "We'd like to have the children get to know their teachers. We want there to be a bond between the teacher and the child. We need the parents to please maintain a distance until we call for them." In other words, "we don't want you here." So this affected the parents who, instead of helping the teachers with their work, left. We had a group of parents at The Learning Academy, but with so many prerequisites she got rid of us. No. There is a big problem at The Learning Academy. The principal doesn't accept any visitors. No. She can't. She's too busy to see anybody.

During my career as a teacher in San Diego I met a very dynamic Latina mother who had a history of many years of activism and involvement at her children's school, and she painted a similar picture. At the time I met her she was serving on the school's governance team as well as the school site council. During one of our discussions she recounted some of her own experiences with an ex-administrator at her child's school and the attempts this administrator would make to preclude her and the other Latino parents' active participation. She related how the principal would meet with the parents at the school during monthly Parent Coffee events but would not be willing to engage their concerns or answer questions.

> The parents are completely denied. One of the main barriers that we had at the school was "time" because they would give us parent meetings but only to inform us about what she (the principal) wanted to tell us. She would give us the meetings, but she would be the only one allowed to speak. When we had questions, [she would say], "I'm sorry but I have to leave. I need to be in a classroom at such and such time." The meeting would end. We'd be left with all our unanswered questions.

The concerns that were voiced by these mothers (as well as many other parents and teachers I have worked with) present an interesting pattern in how administrators relate to active parents, or at least active low-income bicultural parents. For the most part, administrators appear to have an extreme loyalty to the school system rather than to their constituents, which are the parents and the community. Thus, according to the many parent comments I have heard throughout the years it appears that the administrators in many cases acted as not only barriers but at times as counter-resistance to their efforts to improve their children's schools.

From the parents' comments and my experiences working with them, I suggest that the process of involving bicultural parents in the school system is deeply regulated through a procedural network of bureaucracy which functions as a barrier for those who may wish to become more involved in the school system. This process of regulations, protocols, and procedures is further complicated by the issues of language, culture, and class. Parents who do not speak English or possess the political and economic clout to be heard often get discouraged by institutional barriers that become present in the school system as it attempts to protect itself from disruption. Moreover, this bureaucracy and the administrators' blind loyalty to this system effectively work to squelch any concerns or opposition bicultural parents may have.

The Need to Understand Bicultural Parent Resistance

The purpose of this chapter has been to provide an alternative perspective for understanding the low levels of bicultural parent participation in the schools. This point of view contradicts the commonly held assumption that bicultural parents do not participate in their children's schools because they are either disinterested or incapable. It presents a theoretical construct which will help us analyze, examine, and reflect upon the sources of resistance which in turn "can provide the incentive for powerful social and self-transformation that leaves one's sense of identity in place."[17]

The modes of resistance bicultural parents explicitly and implicitly exhibit also demonstrate their awareness of the contradictions present in their involvement in the schools. Therefore, within the school context, "in its broadest sense, resistance arises out of the conflicts and contradictions between a person's lived experience and the ideologies of knowledge and power cultivated by the dominant culture and expressed in the schooling process."[18] Thus, in our attempt to understand why bicultural parents do not participate in the public schools in high numbers, resistance must figure significantly in our understanding of what we can do to transform the root causes of oppressive social and school conditions so that the public education system can begin to truly serve the needs of all children and communities.

Critical Incident

A group of 28 Latino parents are outside of a school picketing. The school is 70% Latino, 8% white and 22% African-American. The parents are demanding the removal of the principal from the school.

Their argument is that the principal is culturally insensitive and creates obstacles for parents and teachers who support bilingual education. The parents and selected bilingual teachers seek a program that promotes high levels of literacy in English and in Spanish for the new academic year. The program being provided at the start of the year is only offered in kindergarten with the remaining grades offering sheltered English instruction. The parents believe that the goal of the school's current program is to teach the English Learners the minimal threshold of English so that they can be transitioned to English-only classrooms as soon as possible.

The parents decide to picket on a Tuesday September morning. Many other parents walk by them as they drop their children off at school. The white and African-American parents pretty much ignore the commotion since they do not understand what the issue is about. Besides, their children are not participating in bilingual programs so the matter doesn't affect them. Some Latino parents stop to talk to the picketing parents yet the majority walks by them. Some are heard murmuring that these are the same parents that are always causing trouble at the school and that they are just "troublemakers" who are never satisfied with anything the principal does.

At the end of the event, the picketing parents are discouraged that many parents appeared to be disinterested or even hostile to their message. They question their strategy and if they should continue their picketing. Several of the parents feel that perhaps they should just pull their children out of this school since the other parents do not appear to support their efforts.

Questions for Reflection
1. What is the problem in this scenario?
2. What are the possible conditions contributing to the problem?
3. Are the picketing parents in the right? In the wrong?
4. What options, alternatives, or solutions can the parents do to resolve the problem? What can the school personnel do?
5. What else can the picketing parents do to get their message across to the other parents?
6. Are the picketing parents demonstrating a level of resistance? Are the other parents? Identify those forms of resistance.

A Paradigm of Tension, Contradiction, and Resistance

Within the public education system there is an ever-present struggle for power, and ultimately humanity, between bicultural communities and the schools that serve them. Deeply rooted within this struggle are conflicting interests and contradictory assumptions on the part of the school system that preclude the success of low-income bicultural students as well as the authentic participation of their parents. In order to understand this conflict, I propose a Paradigm of Tension, Contradiction, and Resistance (Figure 1). This framework takes into account the socioeconomic and historical factors discussed in the previous chapters as a means of studying the relationship between bicultural parents and the institution of public education. This framework lays out a general roadmap for viewing the socioeconomic and historical influences which affect the relationship between low-income bicultural parents and school personnel. In general, I argue that the relationship between bicultural parents and the public school system is neither exclusively limited to the school campus nor to the individuals who comprise the school community. To the contrary, the relationship between bicultural parents and the school system is a micro-reflection of societal contradictions and tensions in the areas of economic exploitation and racism.

This framework also argues that resistance, or conflict, figures significantly in how low-income bicultural parents relate to oppressive school policies and practices and that this resistance can take separate courses. This resistance has the potential to be empowering and transformational, in that it can promote authentic change within the system, making it more responsive and democratic; or, it can be oppressive and self-defeating, in that it simply helps recreate the existing structure and/or conditions that fed the resistance in the first place. And finally, I argue that one of the goals of authentic parental involvement in the schools is to help parents and educators reflect upon and understand their role within this paradigm of tension, contradiction, and resistance and how to choose the paths which will be most beneficial to them, their children, their community, and to society in general.

In this brief chapter I will elaborate more on this framework as we near our conclusion in which I will lay out potential elements for establishing a more transformational paradigm of parent involvement.

Tensions and Contradictions

Our society and thus our institutions are rife with contradictions. These contradictions are rooted at the macro-levels of capitalism and race relations, or in more direct terms: economic exploitation and white supremacy. These two constructs form the foundations on which our country is based and influence our ideology and our actions at differing levels of social interaction. These constructs are therefore deeply embedded in the school system and in the relationship between parents and representatives of the institution.

Persell[1] establishes a useful *structure of dominance* framework that takes into account variables at four levels of analysis, *Societal, Institutional, Interpersonal,* and *Intrapersonal,* for analyzing inequitable educational outcomes, thus social inequities. Her framework provides a practical starting point for the very reason that it forces us to look at social inequities and contradictions through various lenses and at various levels, though always rooted in the socioeconomic environment. My paradigm is influenced by Persell's work in that the root of the problem for low levels of bicultural parental participation are found in socioeconomic and historical factors which have maintained the current system of domination and the fact that the school system is one of the primary institutions that contributes to social reproduction. In simple terms, the contradictions found in the school system are merely micro-reflections of societal contradictions and tensions.

The contradictions that come to fore at the societal level are often expressed in three basic categories: *class, gender, and race.* These three factors become the basis of discrimination and social reproduction. We constantly witness class struggles (though not as apparent in the U.S. as in other countries) in which poor, low-income, and working-class citizens struggle to maintain a foothold in our capitalist society in attempts to make a living wage and to have a voice in our democracy. Always at a disadvantage, these subordinate groups are prevented from building a common movement of similar class interests however, as they are constantly divided along racial and gender lines. Race and gender issues (including sexual orientation) thus become viewed as separate struggles when actually they are intimately tied to class relations.

As mentioned previously, most of society is inherently oblivious to these social contradictions and they often go unchallenged. There are two general reasons for this. First, there are certain mechanisms at play which obfuscate these contradictions, and secondly, the thoughts and actions of individuals often reflect a non-critical stance which allows these inequities to go unquestioned. These same issues are at play in the school system. The overall inequities of the school system are often rationalized on the basis of deficit thinking and meritocracy, placing the blame on the individual and his or her social group and perpetuated by school personnel who accept and carry on these inequities rather than challenge them. Yet, not everybody is oblivious to these inequities or contradictions. No, there are many people who "sense" there is something wrong, yet they often lack the critical consciousness to name it. These are the embedded tensions that underlie many of the relations and processes of socialization around which we construct meaning.

The dissonance which surrounds our existence as human beings is ever present, yet only a small number of individuals are able to use it as a process for self and social transformation. Few are the individuals that use counter-hegemonic practices in their daily lives and fewer are the teachers who use them in their teaching practices and interpersonal relationships with low-income bicultural children and their communities.

Tensions in Bicultural Parent Involvement

I laid out in a previous chapter that there are embedded tensions in the relationship between bicultural communities and the school personnel in the public school setting. These tensions are ever present in *any* school, even in those in which there appears to be no apparent parental dissatisfaction and where school personnel *seem* to "get along" with the parents. I positioned these tensions in the school personnel's views about culture and knowledge and in their power relations with bicultural parent communities. I argued that school personnel, as a reflection of broader society, tend to hold certain deficit views about bicultural parents in regard to culture and knowledge, as if these groups are somehow lacking and incomplete, thus their interactions reflect a paternalistic orientation in which bicultural parents are to be contained and "educated" using coercive power relations.

Essentially, the culture of the school is that of the broader society. Schools function under the same myths of meritocracy, equal opportunity, and neutrality as does our nation. These myths implant themselves into the mindsets of the school personnel who then use them to define the roles of bicultural parents and students in the school system. Teachers and administrators therefore assume that students and parents who are African-American, Latino, low-income, immigrant, non-English speaking, etc. are somehow exclusively responsible for their academic and social achievement (and failure). Bicultural parents, on the other hand, while not necessarily disagreeing with the myths, at times challenge these views, either passively or actively.

I explained in the previous chapter that the dissonance bicultural parents experience between what the schools claim to value and what they actually experience causes them to resist. This resistance takes on many manifestations, depending on the individual's or group's level of political consciousness and desire to transform the system. For the most part, a large sector of bicultural parents chooses to simply avoid the oppressive situation, thus they refuse to be present at the school. This absence of bicultural parents, however, rather than transforming oppressive school policies and practices, validates the school personnel's assumptions about them—that they are apathetic. Yet, when bicultural parents *do* begin to demonstrate interest in more meaningful and active ways, school personnel keep them under close surveillance, assuring that they don't overstep their bounds, hence the dialectic nature of the contradictions, tensions, and resistance in bicultural parent involvement.

The Dialectical Nature of Contradictions and Resistance

Significant to understanding the relationship between bicultural parents and the institution of public education within the paradigm I propose is the notion that the contradictions inherent in society, its institutions, and in people, are dialectical in nature.

According to the words of Darder, this "dialectical view begins with the fact of human existence and the contradictions and disjunctions that, in part, shape it and make problematic its meaning in the world."[2] McLaren, for his part, adds the following:

> [We must seek out] theories which recognize the problems of society as more than simply isolated events of individuals or deficiencies in the social structure. Rather, these problems are part of the *interactive context* between the individual and society. The individual, a social actor, both creates and is created by the social universe of which he/she is part. Neither the individual nor society is given priority in analysis; the two are inextricably interwoven, so that reference to one must by implication mean reference to the other.[3]

In essence what is being argued here is that the societal contradictions put forth thus far cannot be recognized as idle phenomena. Indeed, as mentioned earlier, society does not act upon the individual in a deterministic fashion. Instead, individuals and social groups are both the product and the maker of society and history. The contradictions found in society are therefore contradictions also found within individuals. Hence:

> Dialectical thought seeks out these social contradictions and sets up a process of open and thoughtful questioning that requires reflection to ensue back and forth between the parts and the whole, the object and the subject, knowledge and human action, process and product, so that further contradictions may be discovered.[4]

What this means for our study of bicultural parents and the schools is that there are different modes of responsibility and accountability in the academic achievement of students of color and the integration of their parents in the school system. It further implies that while the school system has a significant advantage of hegemonic status and power to contain bicultural parents, these parents must also assume an active role in transforming this system so that it meets the needs of not only their children but of their communities as well. Therefore, the plight of bicultural communities within the education system is not one of complete despair, rather particular school policies and practices as well as individual and collective actions on the part of the agents (i.e., parents, students, administrators, and teachers) can promote more "democratic" schools.

Bicultural Parents, Tensions, Contradictions, and Resistance

We must make a distinction between what constitutes "authentic" and "inauthentic" parent involvement in order to understand the tensions that are present in the schools. Moreover, we must identify those practices within schools which function to preclude the academic success of children of color and the meaningful involvement of their parents and communities in order to begin to conceptualize the possibilities of having bicultural parents involved at the schools at levels that will transform the public school system to finally serve their children's interests.

Transforming the school system suggests that efforts must be made to critically engage ideologies and practices that impede a collaborative and authentic relationship between the public school system and bicultural communities. This involves critiquing policies and practices currently found in the public education system, policies which reflect the inequities and coercive "power relations in the broader society."[5] This also means that parents and educators must delve deeper into often-unexplored areas of parent involvement, particularly those related to class, race, and gender, in order to weed out the contradictions and expose them for what they are. Therefore, I put forth that parent involvement must be redefined using a paradigm that will provide the space for voice, access, and the democratic participation of subordinate communities in the process of education.

I pointed out earlier that a fundamental flaw found in the current parent involvement rhetoric is the multiple definitions given to the concept and the fact that there is no consistent agreement on what parent involvement means, though traditionally the inclusion of parents in the school system has been construed by educators to mean parents supporting, not questioning or critiquing, the teachers' academic efforts in educating their children. As a result, assumptions embedded in involving ethnically diverse parents in the education system are complicated and have resulted in considerable tensions among stakeholders.

Tension can best be understood in two simple conceptualizations of "negative tension" and "positive tension." The former is that tension which derives from the social and institutional contradictions which serve to disempower and subjugate bicultural communities. This tension is present due to the dissonance bicultural individuals and groups encounter as they attempt to navigate what is believed to be a neutral educational institution but come face to face with a highly political micro-reflection of broader relationships of domination and coercive power relations.

Positive tension refers to those instances in which historically disempowered groups disrupt the dominant institutions to make way for alternative ways of thinking and living. Specifically, parent involvement in my framework is the personal and collective process of empowerment and critical understanding of broader society and the function of its institutions. It is the linking of social and civic action to that of education advocacy. Consequently, it requires individuals to take critical actions in the task of unmasking these contradictions so that they become apparent to the school community. Indeed, ultimately the level of parent involvement cannot be determined by parent interest or measured by parent presence; rather its success must be determined by whether or not the parents and the community have a voice in their collective future and in that of their children.

To conclude, I propose this paradigm to challenge past research which has by and large been centered on identifying those factors within low-income bicultural families which preclude their children's academic and social success and which has been focused on identifying levels and scopes of involvement that in essence do nothing to change the school or the school system but rather work only to promote the idle attendance of parents at school functions. As a result, what I also propose is that the questions of school effectiveness as opposed to home improvement must also be the focus of scrutiny so that bicultural communities can turn the tables on those researchers, policymakers, and institutional agents which have for many years scrutinized and dissected them. In other words, it is time for bicultural parents to study those in power in order to uncover their ideologies and goals.

Critical Incident

Mr. Allen is the principal of Shelly Elementary School. Shelly Elementary is a small school comprised primarily of immigrant Latino parents in a low-income neighborhood. On this particular afternoon he is receiving a special recognition from the district for having the "highest level of parent participation" in the district.

To the outside visitor, Shelly Elementary is indeed teeming with activity. There are, for example, parent volunteers who help out with recess and lunch duty on a daily basis. There is a high level of participation at the site level advisory committees and at the monthly informational parent meetings with the principal. In addition, there is a Parent Center where parents gather daily to learn about educational and social opportunities, such as health fairs, English classes, citizenship classes, free legal advice, etc., and where teachers daily drop off work that needs be done for their classrooms, such as cutting paper, preparing homework packets, etc. Every year there is also a large parent recognition assembly in which all the parents who participated throughout the year are awarded certificates for their participation.

All in all, Mr. Allen is to be commended for his dedication to making parents feel welcomed at the school, and on this particular afternoon his hard work is being recognized.

Questions for Reflection

1. What are some of the positive aspects of Mr. Allen's parent involvement practices?
2. At what levels of participation do you see the parents participating?
3. What are some further steps Mr. Allen can take to promote a "deeper level" of parent involvement?
4. What are some possible consequences Mr. Allen could face should he promote parent activism and his parents end up becoming "vocal" within the school and the district?

Transformative Parent Involvement

There is a strong consensus among many in the field of education that involving parents in their children's formal education is beneficial to student success, particularly if the students come from historically disenfranchised groups. Yet, despite this stated enthusiasm for involving parents, educators must ask themselves, why is it that the public school system has consistently been unsuccessful in establishing an authentic relationship with the communities it serves, particularly the "hard to reach" parents? Moreover, why is it that teachers who work in many urban and bicultural school settings still find themselves asking: why aren't these parents more involved? Or, why don't these parents care? And, finally, why do bicultural parents who *do* participate often feel that their participation is meaningless or disingenuous?

This chapter will help summarize the issues I have presented thus far in order to help develop a more transformational way of looking at this problem. Included within this chapter is a critique of traditional models, mindsets, and policies which have historically dictated how bicultural parents are to function, and have functioned, within the school system at the level of low-impact rhetoric and volunteerism and to advocate and promote a more genuine, authentic, and meaningful form of democratic parent participation, one that is closely tied to civic activism and social transformation.

This framework of parent involvement is what I refer to as a Transformational Paradigm of Parent Involvement.[1] This paradigm for parent involvement is not a "model" in the sense that it can be replicated on the basis of strategies and techniques; rather it is a general theoretical framework that seeks to pose questions and possible paths that would lead to a more meaningful form of parental participation and voice where parents and teachers develop the tools to understand their social and historical context. It is my belief that the paradigm Ochoa and I propose will serve as an initial step to not only transform the parents' personal self-perception of efficacy and empowerment but also provide the necessary steps towards transforming the schools, the school system, and society as well.

Parent Involvement Models

This chapter's purpose is to propose a more functional and transformational view of parent involvement, one that offers historically disempowered parents the opportunity to become meaningful and active participants in the education of their children. I offer this parent involvement paradigm with the purpose of moving bicultural parents from the passive roles they have generally had in the school system to that of action researchers and decision-makers. This paradigm therefore seeks to redefine the purpose of parent involvement to be much more than individual student achievement or school test scores, as important and necessary that these may be. To do this, I will first provide a critique and overview of what I call traditional parent involvement models. These "models" form the foundation of where we have been with parent involvement and where we still continue to struggle.

I identify the four parent involvement models as: *The Family Influence Model, The Alternative School Reform Model, The Cooperative Schools Model,* and *The Transformative Education Context Model.* These are umbrella terms to identify a line of reasoning and a series of practices used for involving parents, thus while they are not really "models," I will refer to them as such.

Each of the four models has assumptions that perceive parents as either having a passive or active voice or role in the school context. In the examination of these parent involvement models it is possible for common practices from one model to carry over to others. Additionally, it is possible that these models be implemented in various ways according to the school administrator and the particular schools' culture. Nonetheless, using these four models one can recognize the underlying ideology and outcome of each.[2]

The Family Influence Model (I), also referred to as the *Schools Transmission Model,* employs techniques and strategies based on research and ideologies that presume school-related difficulty originates in the family. Since school personnel see the deficiency in learning as originating in the home, changing the home culture becomes the goal of academic interventions. The personnel's belief is that the home culture of the bicultural student is somehow inadequately supporting their academic progress; therefore it must be changed and/or corrected so that the child's life chances are improved. In other words, "[academic] deficiencies are presumed to be corrected by school-designed interventions that make home socialization congruent with the school culture."[3]

The Family Influence Model is founded on the principles of deficit thinking, thinking which views bicultural communities as "lacking" or deficient in intelligence, culture, and/or social adjustment. The underlying assumption of viewing the bicultural parent as a hindrance instead of an asset can be seen in the parent education classes that are often offered by the school in which "parents are given guidelines, materials, and/or trainings to carry out school-like activities in the home."[4] Equally popular are efforts aimed at teaching parents about "effective" parenting and the legitimacy of the school culture.

The overall goal of this model is for the school to provide opportunities for the parents to improve their home condition in order to mirror that of the school culture. No attention is paid to other factors (both inside and outside the school) that contribute to limiting the bicultural community's ability to effectively participate in the schooling process of their children. Furthermore, school personnel are seen as the owners and sources of legitimate knowledge and culture, thus putting forth the notion that bicultural communities have nothing of value to offer. Ironically, despite the obvious shortcoming and disrespect this model has for all communities, particularly bicultural, it continues to be the most commonly accepted among America's public schools.

Alternative School Reform Model (II): This second model provides a shift in paradigm to the Family Influence Model in that the parents and the community try "to change the schools to make them more responsive" to them and their children.[5] This is done by parents exercising their power at the school and challenging school personnel to be more accountable to their children's needs, often through participation on school governance committees and advisory boards. Thus, this model's focus is on the parents' influence in the production of education at the schools.

An underlying assumption behind this model is that the schools will actually heed the parents' suggestions and input. Thus, it is

important to note that this model is more prevalent, and more effective, amongst communities from the dominant culture. That is, mid-
dle- and upper-class white parents have more success in demanding
their children's educational rights than do bicultural parents of lower
resources. This is due to the fact that there is a closer symmetrical
power and status relationship and because these parents know their
rights within the schooling process, and have the ability to communi-
cate their demands. Furthermore, more affluent parents have the
ability to hold school officials accountable.

The Cooperative Systems Model (III): This model is all-encompassing
and general in that it integrates the parents into various roles within
the school, even as employees (lunch duty helpers, teachers' assis-
tants, etc.). It sees the parent as a volunteer, paid employee, teacher at
home, audience, decision-maker, and adult learner. The Cooperative
Systems Model therefore attempts to integrate the economic, social,
and educational interests of the parents under one general umbrella
term of parent involvement. The philosophy behind this third model
argues that "cooperation between the two institutions of the family
and the school exists."[6]

The multiple roles parents occupy within the school, particularly
that of a paid employee, makes direct parent advocacy less likely in
this model, however, since those who are working in the school have
developed an economic interest in the continuation of the status quo
education system since it is the source of their livelihood. Furthermore, parents who challenge the school system and are active players
in school activities are often co-opted by becoming employees of the
school who then must adhere to its existing practices. Finally, for
bicultural parents, taking multiple roles in the school assumes that
there is truly an authentic shared power structure within it, which
contradicts the experiences of many of these parents who acknowledge that their roles at the school are for the most part symbolic.

The Transformative Education Context Model (IV): This fourth model
is based on the notion that knowledge is socially constructed between
participants, and as such, all are equally responsible and capable of
contributing, understanding, and transforming the educational process.[7] Influenced by the work of Freire, Giroux, Cummins, and other
critical pedagogues, this model's philosophy argues that "through
analysis and critique, all people are capable of engaging in actions
that may transform their present realities."[8] Parent involvement is

seen as a process of transformation in which social literacy and critical consciousness is achieved by all the participants for the benefit of student literacy, academic achievement, and school and social transformation. This process of transformation is possible via the Freirian principles of dialogue and problem-posing education that seek to name the problem, understand the conditions creating the problem, and offer alternatives and solutions to the problems.

Darder writes about the "unwavering support that critical educators have for the Freirian notion of dialogue as an emancipatory educational process."[9] Such support is grounded in the belief that dialogue is important in that it provides the generative themes, or the dominant school and community issues, that are necessary for relevant learning as well as a vehicle for consciousness-raising. In addition, dialogue promotes a language of not only resistance but of possibility. The possibility for positive change is rooted in the belief that collaboration within the entire school population will build a community of learners in which learning is not isolated, but collective, historical, social, authentic, and transformational. Thus, bicultural parents act to promote their interests, those of their children, and those of other people's children, while at the same time participating in the political process of changing their lives from objects to subjects, or from passive to active involvement.

By now, the questions raised by the reader might be: how is this model of parent participation different from the previous models, besides the rhetoric? Also, isn't this model merely based on utopian thinking and ivory tower philosophizing? Moreover, is this model even possible and has it functioned elsewhere before?

First and foremost, the importance of this model is its ability to take into account the social, cultural, and economic factors impacting the quality of life of the school community and of the students. The Transformative Education Context Model addresses the issue of how knowledge is constructed and normalized based on an individual's or group's position in society. Additionally, it does not ignore or conceal the strong political interests found in schooling. Therefore, parent involvement is seen as political and active. In other words, parent involvement is a political process in which parents from diverse backgrounds (including middle-class whites) work to transform a system that engenders subordination and stratifies students. Furthermore, it presents a counter-perspective which views the home knowledge and culture of the participants as equally valid and powerful for social change. It is this "model" that forms the basis of the Olivos and Ochoa paradigm,[10] a paradigm that seeks to transform parent involvement into a meaningful act of empowerment and political involvement with the goal of making education a democratic and reflective action.

The Parent Involvement Analysis Paradigm, as depicted in Table 1, illustrates a formula Ochoa and I propose for analyzing progressive levels of parent involvement in a democratic social and educational context. The paradigm assumes that movement from one system to another is driven by the social commitment and developmental consciousness of its participants and communities. The paradigm provides a progressive and developmental course towards socioeconomic and political consciousness. The paradigm begins and moves from a functionalist philosophical/ideological perspective (Level I), to a structural functionalist (Level II), to a conflict theory (Level III), and finally to a combined use of conflict theory and interpretivist social-constructionist perspectives to create socioeconomically and politically pluralistic school communities.

Level I of parent involvement, for example, centers on ensuring that the parent community conforms to the dominant values of the school's culture or in support of the status quo (functionalist). Feinberg and Soltis[11] define the functionalist perspective as serving to socialize parents and students to adapt to the economic, political, and social institutions of that society. In this perspective, functionalists suggest that we view social institutions as analogous to the parts of the body. Each part functions to serve the needs and purpose of the whole. Thus, Level I involvement is simply concerned with superficially connecting the parent community to the school in order for them to conform to its culture, which often leads to a passive school community.

Level II of the paradigm of parent involvement is guided by the focus on assimilating the parent community to the dominant values of the school's culture or in support of governing rules (structural functionalist). Under this perspective, schooling is seen as a means of socialization for molding the school community to fit existing social practices and requirements. The perspective here is to view equity as simply providing the same resources to all participants without concern for its benefits or utility. This view's only concern is thus providing limited resources, and it is the responsibility of the participants to fit into these available resources. Quality, relevance and meaningfulness are not criteria for determining benefit or utility of access. As a result, Level II is simply concerned with working with the parent community to collaborate in support of the school's culture in order to take advantage of its available services and without questioning its policies, programs, staffing practices, or standards.

Level	Theoretical /Social Focus	Parent Involvement Models	Perception of Parents as Contributors to Schools
I Status quo	Functionalist (Conformity)	Family influence: Change bicultural parents—"improve" home condition for participants to acquire preferred behaviors and values	Superficially connecting parents to school culture (I)
II	Structural functionalist (Social control and harmony)	Cooperative systems: parents participate within the school culture to assimilate to school practices and behaviors	Parents as collaborators of school culture (II)
III	Conflict theory (Equity and power)	Alternative school reform: Parents challenge schools to be more responsive, inclusive and equitable	Parents as co-participants in the decision-making process (III)
IV Open Democratic system	Conflict theory, social constructionist, & interpretivist (Transformational change towards cultural and economic democracy)	Transformational education: Problem-posing that seeks solutions enabling inclusion, voice and representation in decision making	Cultural democracy, parents as action researchers, agents of transformative change in the school and community (IV)

Table 1. Parent Involvement Analysis Paradigm

Level III of the paradigm of parent involvement focuses on addressing social and educational inequities that have been created by the dominant culture and embedded in the practices of the school's culture (conflict theory). Under this perspective, the view of schooling is seen as a social practice supported and utilized by those in power to maintain the culture of dominance in the social order. This perspective questions the inequitable class relations in society and urges social action against undue schooling which functions as an instrument of class domination, serving to produce the workforce and maintain class relationships.

From a legal perspective, the conflict theorist perspective represents legal and civil rights legislation that advocates eradicating past discriminatory practices through social and educational institutions that seek to actualize the principle of "equal benefits." This principle is not only concerned with access to resources but also with the quality of services to develop the human condition. The responsibility shifts from the individual to institutional services to fit the needs of its participants. Quality, relevance and meaningfulness become the criteria for assessing benefit or utility of access. Consequently, Level III is concerned with the parent community becoming a co-participant in the decision making process of the school while seeking the full benefits of the educational system and special programs which are created to provide equal benefits.

Level IV of the paradigm combines the equity focus of the conflict theorist perspective, the emphasis of the constructivist perspective in seeking an involvement process that promotes parent and student participants in the construction of knowledge, dialogue, and as agents of creating and recreating meaning in the improvement of the school community, and the interpretivist perspective that sees the social world as a world made up of purposeful actors, who acquire, share, and interpret a set of meanings, rules, and norms that make social interaction possible. The focus is on creating culturally democratic participation in developing and implementing social and educational policy that develops social responsibility and the human condition— socially, cognitively, and politically.

Participants in this level have a deep understanding of social inequality and a social justice orientation in seeking to act on social injustice at the personal and community level. From a legal perspective, the combined perspectives seek to operationalize cultural democracy (equal representation, equal participation, equal access, equal encouragement, and the right to social mobility) while directly addressing practices that eliminate racial and class preference. This perspective also seeks to transform the school community to ensure that its values and practices are congruent with the pursuit of cultural and economic democracy. Democratic education is both a means and an end.[12] The means is informed debate leading to reflective action; the ends are a society where decisions are made on the basis of universal participation in informed action; where the majority rules only to the extent that specified rights of minorities are respected; and where the decisions made equally encourage all members of the society to fully participate in every facet of the society. Accordingly, Level IV is concerned with creating a school community for the "collective we."

Level I to level IV suggest educational practices (parent involvement) that move from an authoritarian model of governance to a democratic model of governance and work. The paradigm also places the parent involvement models mentioned earlier into a context that will serve to propose the direction that we need to direct our efforts as we seek socio-economic-political pluralism in our democracy. The objective of the Olivos and Ochoa parent involvement paradigm is to reach the fourth level of transformational education that is guided by parental participatory involvement. Such involvement ensures the participation of low-income parents and can be viewed as consisting of five interrelated parts as seen in Figure 5.

First it is initiated through a problem-posing that forms the basis of our inquiry and work. Second, through this process of inquiry and dialogue, participants reflect to learn about the world and about themselves and thus engage in a transformative educational experience. Third, participants conceptualize the goals of their involvement and commitment to improve and create the social conditions necessary for a more democratic involvement. Fourth, through personal and individual and collective reflection, action is taken toward resolving the issues that initiated the problem-posing process.[13] And fifth, these concepts are internalized which lead to further problem-posing and reflection.

It is through this act of questioning and inquiry that a true educational act occurs, and knowledge is invented or re-invented in community with others. According to Freire, "Education as a practice of freedom—as opposed to education as the practice of domination—denies that [we are] abstract isolated, independent and unattached to the world."[14] Figure 5 provides the circular process of problem-posing and reflection.

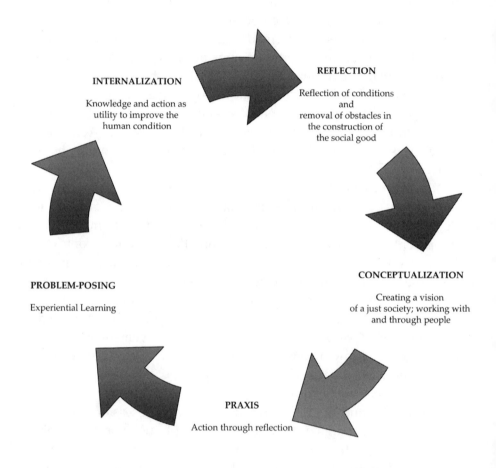

Figure 5: Problem-posing and Reflection

In problem-posing dialogue, participants come to recognize their ability to know and to reflect. Parent involvement is based on empowerment that leads to action and further reflection, which, in turn, leads to further questions for inquiry and action research.[15] We see knowledge in its action, practice and reflection. In the words of the

Maturana and Varela, "Reflection is the process of knowing how we know. It is [the] only chance we have to discover our blindness and to recognize that the certainties and knowledge of others are, respectively, as overwhelming and tenuous as our own."[16]

This paradigm on parent involvement therefore ultimately seeks to pursue the ideal of cultural democracy. Such an ideal exists where the principle of equal encouragement is institutionalized in policies and practices that unmask and eliminate discriminatory racial and class institutional policies and practices. The institution attains cultural democracy when its infrastructure is reflective of the total community at all structural levels of the organization. At this point, multi-racial competency becomes the norm. Cultural democracy recognizes the existence of racial and class tensions as a necessary condition of its existence and for actualizing democracy.[17]

Another essential process of transformational education in the paradigm is participatory research as a way for researchers and disempowered people to meet in collaboration to address concrete and specific problems and situations. This participatory research means working with and through people as a viable tool in discussing issues of social justice and equity through the following:

1. The active participation of the individuals or groups who have an interest in changing the conditions in which they live or work.
2. The researcher (parent/teacher/administrator/university faculty) and the participants collectively exploring those conditions, which may be oppressive in nature and promote a lack of equity in education.
3. Through this process the researchers do not maintain a position of power over the participants or promote his/her ideas about the world.
4. The researcher does not define knowledge for the participants; rather knowledge is derived from the collective activity of dialogue and work.
5. The researchers and the participants engage in dialogues to facilitate both a deeper understanding of the problems surrounding the research and an exploration of some type of solution or structural change.

6. The process calls for engagement and working with and through people.

7. The researchers and the participants constantly reflect on the challenges of current educational and social problems.

8. The researchers and the participants engage in dialogical activity that explores the question of research, its use and how it serves to support the selected communities.

9. The researchers and the participants work with communities to improve the human conditions through transformational approaches that do not blame but rather seek structural solutions. The result is a dynamic process in the development of a plan for action for the participants to transform their world.

10. Transformation will not occur unless the co-researchers name their realities and then take action to improve them for themselves and others with similar realities. The act of taking theory, critical reflection through engagement in a free and open manner with social action is defined as praxis.

The outcome of participatory research is to engage researchers and community in the process of praxis to transform oppressive conditions into opportunities to recreate conditions of hope, love, humility, and social justice. Therefore, the objective behind this parent involvement paradigm is to examine the nature and cause of poverty, oppression, and exploitation and to seek action to resolve the problems and empower the participating community and transform social realities in order to achieve social justice.

Bicultural Parents Transforming the Public Schools

The greatest challenge of operationalizing a model such as the one Ochoa and I propose is visualizing its possibilities. To visualize these possibilities one must understand that there are many parents and parent groups currently out in the public school system that have already taken their own individual steps toward a transformational view of being involved in their children's schools. These movements demonstrate how bicultural parents have come to understand their position in society and to pose problems and questions as to why these inequities exist. This problem-posing is done with the purpose of seeking solutions that will benefit the entire school community.

Conclusion

My experiences of working with bicultural parents indicate to me that they are not oblivious to the injustices found in the public school system. Many of them are convinced that they too must participate actively in the struggle for educational justice. What is lacking, however, is a culture of collaboration and solidarity between them and the educators that serve their children that will reshape their destiny and transform the school system to meet their needs and highlight their strengths. For far too long educators have been distanced and suspicious of bicultural parents, diverted from understanding the power they possess as agents of change and social transformation.

I contend that there is a need to transform the public schools so that they meet the needs of all children, particularly those who have historically been neglected by this system. Understanding the important role bicultural parents play in their children's lives I have attempted to demonstrate the urgency of developing a transformational paradigm of parent involvement using a participatory and problem-posing approach. I believe that parents hold a fundamental interest in having the schools succeed: the academic and social success of their children; therefore, I offered a critique of how parents, particularly bicultural ones, have traditionally been asked to participate in their children's schools.

All too often bicultural parents have been invited into the schools using models and approaches which have been contradictory to their authentic involvement. Thus, I put forward in this book that until bicultural parents are invited into the schools with the understanding that they and the educators that serve their children share the equal responsibility and power to transform the schools, the school system will continue to confront what is quite possibly this nation's greatest contradiction, the inability to close the educational achievement disparity between specific social. groups. Therefore, I propose that a transformational paradigm of parent involvement must be actualized so that bicultural parents, the teachers that teach their children, and bicultural communities can work together to generate the conditions that will create an equitable and democratic schooling experience and society.

For teachers who work in bicultural communities, the lessons learned in this book point to the urgency of reflecting on past practices and hidden ideological biases imposed on them by their own schooling experiences and traditional teacher preparation programs. Their engagement with bicultural parents should therefore become a liberating act of humanization and transformation. One cannot merely stand idly by watching as low-income bicultural parents struggle alone to protect the future of their children in a school system that is domineering and exploitative. Educators, teachers and administrators must step forward and carve out ways of authentically and democratically engaging bicultural parents in a manner that will once and for all put an end to a dehumanizing relationship that belittles those whom society has deemed dispensable.

Finally, the recommendations put forth in this book do not constitute a cookie-cutter model for bicultural parent engagement but rather a theoretical foundation for developing the space and the language necessary for creating opportunities for struggle and democratic participation in our public schools. This participation will not, however, occur without tension or conflict. Thus, we should not make efforts to avoid them. Indeed, those structures of inequality which constitute the foundation of public schooling in the United States must be challenged by educators and parents who understand the importance of building a political community of advocates that will transform not only the schools but society as well, and tension and conflict figure significantly in that challenge.

Questions for Reflection

1. How has your understanding of parent involvement changed after reading this book?
2. Reflecting back on the case study found in Chapter 1, what elements of "transformative parent involvement" can you identify?
3. What steps can you take within your education setting to promote more "authentic" parent involvement?
4. What are some barriers you might face in your work with bicultural parents?

Notes

Foreword

[1] P. Freire, *The pedagogy of the city*. (New York: Continuum, 1993), p. 24.

[2] G. Orfield, *Schools more separate: Consequences of a decade of resegregation.* (July 2001). Available at http://www.civilrightsproject.harvard.edu/research/deseg/Schools_More_Separate.pdf ("[N]ew statistics from the 1998–99 school year show that segregation continued to intensify throughout the 1990s, . . . [f]rom 1988 to 1998, most of the progress of the previous two decades in increasing integration . . . was lost.").

Chapter 1

[1] E.M. Olivos, *Dialectical tensions, contradictions, and resistance: A study of the relationship between Latino parents and the public school system within a socioeconomic "structure of dominance."* (Unpublished doctoral dissertation, San Diego State University/Claremont Graduate University, 2003).

[2] Californians for Justice (CFJ). *First things first: Why we must stop punishing students and fix California's schools. A report on school inequality and the impact of the California high school exit exam.* (Long Beach, CA: CFJ Education Fund, 2003).

[3] All names are pseudonyms.

[4] By "they," Mrs. Cervantes is referring to the more affluent school communities of San Diego.

[5] R. R. Valencia (Ed.), *The evolution of deficit thinking: Educational thought and practice.* (London: The Falmer Press, 1997); R. R. Valencia, & M. S. Black, Mexican Americans don't value education! —On the basis of the myth, mythmaking, and debunking. *The Journal of Latinos and Education*, 1 (2), (2002), 81–103.

[6] These were bi-weekly morning meetings held by the administrators to meet informally with all interested parents.

Chapter 2

[1] See E.M. Olivos, *Dialectical tensions, contradictions, and resistance: A study of the relationship between Latino parents and the public school system within a socioeconomic 'structure of dominance.'* (Unpublished doctoral dissertation, San Diego State University/Claremont Graduate University, 2003); E.M. Olivos, Tensions, contradictions, and resistance: An activist's reflection of the struggles of Latino parents in the public school system. *The High School Journal: Chicana/o Activism in Education: Theories and Pedagogies of Trans/formation*, 87(4), (2004), 25–35; and, E.M. Olivos & A.M. Ochoa, Operationalizing a transformational paradigm of parent involvement in K. Cadiero-Kaplan, A. Ochoa, J. Rodriguez & N.

Kuhlman, (Eds.) *The living work of teachers: Ideology and practice with and in community*. (Los Angeles: California Association for Bilingual Education, in press).

[2] A. Darder, *Culture and power in the classroom: A critical foundation for bicultural education*. (Westport, CT: Bergin & Garvey, 1991), p. xvii.

[3] *Ibid.*, p. 48.

[4] See Darder, 1991, for a similar discussion and her critique of "traditional American pedagogy."

[5] C.H. Persell, *Education and inequality: The roots and results of stratification in America's schools*. (New York: The Free Press, 1977).

[6] See A.T. Henderson & K.L. Mapp, *A new wave of evidence: The impact of school, family and community connections on student achievement*. (Austin, TX: Southwest Educational Development Laboratory, 2002) for an omnibus review of recent literature in parental involvement in education.

[7] C. Jordan, E. Orozco & A. Averett, *Emerging issues in school, family, & community connections*. (Austin, TX: National Center for Family & Community Connections with Schools, 2001), p. viii.

[8] *Ibid.*, p. viii.

[9] Z. Cline & J. Necochea, ¡Basta ya! Latino parents fighting entrenched racism. *Bilingual Research Journal*, 25 (1&2), (2001), 1–26, p. 23.

[10] *Ibid.*, p. 23.

[11] M. Boethel, *Diversity: School, family, & community connections*. (Austin, TX: National Center for Family & Community Connections with Schools, 2003); C. Compton-Lilly, *Confronting racism, poverty, and power: Classroom strategies to change the world*. (Portsmouth, NH: Heinemann, 2004).

[12] U.S. Department of Education. Characteristics of the 100 largest public elementary and secondary school districts in the United States 2001–02. (Washington, D.C.: Institute of Educational Sciences, National Center for Education Statistics (NCEA), 2003)

[13] R. Núñez, *Schools, parents, and empowerment: An ethnographic study of Mexican-origin parents participation in their children's schools*. (Unpublished Doctoral Dissertation, San Diego State University/Claremont Graduate School, San Diego, CA/Claremont, CA, 1994).

[14] C. Delgado-Gaitán, *Literacy for empowerment: The role of parents in children's education*. (New York: The Falmer Press, 1990); Henderson & Mapp; S.P. McCaleb, *Building communities of learners*. (New York: St. Martin's Press, 1994).

[15] R. Clark, *Family life and school achievement: Why poor black children succeed or fail*. (Chicago: The University of Chicago Press, 1983); C. Delgado-Gaitán, 1990; D. Taylor & C. Dorsey-Gaines, *Growing up literate: Learning from inner-city families*. (Portsmouth, NH: Heinemann, 1988); G.R. Lopez, *On whose terms? Understanding involvement through the eyes of migrant parents*. Paper presented at the Annual Meeting of the American Educational Research Association (AERA), Seattle, WA. (2001) as cited in Henderson & Mapp, p. 138.

[16] *Ibid.*, p. 7.

[17] M.A. Lopez. & H. Kreider, Beyond input: Achieving authentic participation in school reform. *Evaluation exchange: A periodical on emerging strategies in evaluating child and families*, IX (2) (Harvard Family Research Project: Harvard Graduate School of Education, 2003); K. Mediratta, N. Fruchter, & A.C. Lewis, *Organizing*

for school reform: How communities are finding their voices and reclaiming their public schools. (New York: Institute for Education and Social Policy, Steinhardt School of Education, New York University, 2002); E. Sullivan, *Civil society and school accountability: A human rights approach to parent and community participation in NYC schools.* (New York: Center for Economic and Social Rights, 2003).
[18] Olivos, 2003.

Chapter 3

[1] J. Cummins, *Negotiating identities: Education for empowerment in a diverse society.* (2nd edition). (Ontario, CA: California Association for Bilingual Education, 2001).
[2] W. Feinberg & J.F. Soltis, *School and society.* (4th edition) (New York: Teachers College Press, 2004), p. 10.
[3] S. Bowles, & H. Gintis, *Schooling in capitalist America: Educational reform and the contradictions of economic life.* (New York: Basic Books, Inc., 1976); P. McLaren, *Life in schools: An introduction to critical pedagogy in the foundation of education.* (4th edition). (Boston: Allyn & Bacon, 2003); C. H. Persell, *Education and inequality: The roots and results of stratification in America's schools.* (New York: The Free Press, 1977).
[4] D. Corson, *Language, minority education and gender: Linking social justice and power.* (Clevedon, England: Multilingual Matters LTD, 1993), p. 5.
[5] Feinberg & Soltis, p. 7.
[6] I.M. Young, *Justice and the politics of difference.* (Princeton, NJ: Princeton University Press, 1990), p. 51.
[7] H. Walberg, & J.L. Bast, *Education and capitalism: How overcoming our fear of markets and economics can improve America's schools.* (Palo Alto, CA: Hoover Institution, 2003), p. 104.
[8] Nobel Laureate economist Robert William Fogel.
[9] Walberg & Bast, p. 105.
[10] Feinberg & Soltis, p. 50.
[11] A. Gramsci, *Selections from the prison notebooks of Antonio Gramsci.* (G.N. Smith, Editor and Translator). (New York: International Publishers, 1997), p. 12.
[12] Marianne de Francia, personal communication, December 6, 2004
[13] S. Shannon, Minority parental involvement: A Mexican mother's experience and a teacher's interpretation. *Education and Urban Society.* 29(1), (1996), 71–84.
[14] Persell, p. 9.
[15] Feinberg & Soltis provide a good analysis of the relationship between schools and society using three theoretical lenses: functionalism, conflict theory, and interpretivism.
[16] The term *structure of dominance* comes from Persell, 1977.
[17] Cummins; Darder; S. Nieto, *Affirming diversity: The sociopolitical context of multicultural education.* (4th edition) (Boston: Pearson Education, Inc., 2004); Persell and many others document how tracking, intelligence testing, teacher expectations, etc. negatively affect bicultural student performance.

[18] Cummins, 2001.

[19] Persell, p. 30.

[20] Marianne de Francia, personal communication, December 6, 2004

[21] D. Spener, Transitional bilingual education and the socialization of immigrants. In P. Leistyna, A. Woodrum, & S. Sherblom (Eds.), *Breaking free: The transformative power of critical pedagogy* (pp. 59-82). (Cambridge, MA: Harvard Educational Review, 1999), p. 59.

[22] S. Bowles, & H. Gintis, p. 102.

[23] Persell, p. 12.

[24] R. Núñez, *Themes on racial factors in education.* (Unpublished doctoral qualifying examination, San Diego State University, 1992), p. 25.

[25] Shannon, p. 72.

[26] Cummins; A. Lareau, & E.M. Horvat, Moments of social inclusion and exclusion: Race, class, and cultural capital in family-school relationships. *Sociology of Education, 72(1),* (1999), 37-53.

[27] G.E. Guerrero, *A study of Mexican American and Anglo parents' relationship with the schools.* (Unpublished Doctoral Dissertation, Harvard University, 1982), p. 23.

[28] Shannon, p. 72.

[29] As cited in R. R. Valencia (Ed.), *The evolution of deficit thinking: Educational thought and practice.* (London: The Falmer Press, 1997), p. 3.

Chapter 4

[1] R. Núñez, *Schools, parents, and empowerment: An ethnographic study of Mexican-origin parents' participation in their children's schools.* (Unpublished Doctoral Dissertation, San Diego State University/Claremont Graduate School, San Diego, CA/Claremont, CA, 1994), p. 55.

[2] *Ibid.,* p. 55.

[3] See S. Bowles, & H. Gintis, *Schooling in capitalist America: Educational reform and the contradictions of economic life.* (New York: Basic Books, Inc., 1976) & C. H. Persell, *Education and inequality: The roots and results of stratification in America's schools.* (New York: The Free Press, 1977) for two very good structural critiques of public schooling.

[4] Persell, p. 7 (italics in original).

[5] M. Barrera, A theory of racial inequality. In A. Darder, R.D. Torres, & H. Gutierrez (Eds). *Latinos and education.* (pp. 3–44). (Notre Dame: University of Notre Dame Press, 1997), p. 31.

[6] Terms used by A. Cintron, *Institutional racism in American society: A primer.* (Human Resource Development Project of the Bureau of Naval Personnel, 1970); Núñez; and Z. Cline & J. Necochea, ¡Basta ya! Latino parents fighting entrenched racism. *Bilingual Research Journal, 25* (1&2), (2001), 1–26, respectively.

[7] Cintron, p. 1.

[8] A. Darder, *Culture and power in the classroom: A critical foundation for bicultural education.* (Westport, CT: Bergin & Garvey, 1991), p. 41.

[9] D. August, & K. Hakuta (Eds.), *Educating language minority children.* (Washington, D.C.: National Academy Press, 1998), p. 35.

[10] Cintron; J. Hitchcock, *Decentering whiteness.* Retrieved May 2, 2005 from the website *Center for the Study of White American Culture,* http://www.euroamerican.org/editorials/Speech1.asp

[11] P. McIntosh, W*hite privilege and male privilege: A personal account of coming to see correspondences through work in women's studies.* (Wellesley, MA: Center for Research on Women, Wellesley College, 1998).

[12] See Darder, 1991.

[13] R. Núñez, *Themes on racial factors in education.* (Unpublished doctoral qualifying examination, San Diego State University, 1992), p. 39.

[14] E.M. Wood, *Democracy against capitalism: Renewing historical materialism.* (Cambridge, MA: Cambridge University Press, 1995), p. 268. (italics in original)

[15] Refer to R. R. Valencia (Ed.), *The evolution of deficit thinking: Educational thought and practice.* (London: The Falmer Press, 1997) for an in-depth discussion on deficit thinking and its influence on educational policy and practice.

[16] M. Barrera, *Race and class in the Southwest: A theory of racial inequality.* Notre Dame: University of Notre Dame Press, 1979), p. 180.

[17] R. R. Valencia, & M. S. Black, Mexican Americans don't value education!—On the basis of the myth, mythmaking, and debunking. *Journal of Latinos and Education,* 1 (2), (2002), 81–103, p. 83.

[18] M. Barrera, A theory of racial inequality. In A. Darder, R.D. Torres, & H. Gutierrez (Eds). *Latinos and education.* (pp. 3–44). (Notre Dame: University of Notre Dame Press, 1997), p. 3.

[19] R.J. Herrnstein, & C. Murray, *The bell curve: intelligence and class structure in American life.* New York: Free Press Paperbacks, 1994); A.R. Jensen, How much can we boost IQ and scholastic achievement? *Harvard Educational Review,* 39, (1969), 1–123.

[20] W. Feinberg & J.F. Soltis, *School and society.* (4th edition) (New York: Teachers College Press, 2004).

[21] N.R. Kuncel, S.A. Hezlett, & D.S. Ones, Academic performance, career potential, creativity, and job performance: Can one construct predict them all? *Journal of Personality and Social Psychology,* 86 (1), (2004), 148–161.

[22] As cited in Barrera, 1997, p. 5.

[23] P. Skerry, *Mexican Americans: The ambivalent minority.* (New York: The Free Press, 1993).

[24] Núñez, p. 14.

[25] J. Cummins, *Negotiating identities: Education for empowerment in a diverse society.* (2nd edition). (Ontario, CA: California Association for Bilingual Education, 2001), p. 8.

[26] E. Trueba, *Latinos unidos: From cultural diversity to the politics of solidarity.* (Lanham, ML: Rowman & Littlefield Publishers Inc., 1999), p. 53 (italics in original).

[27] S. Nieto, *Affirming diversity: The sociopolitical context of multicultural education.* (Boston: Pearson Education, Inc., 2004), p. 39.

[28] *Ibid.,* p. 39.

[29] Núñez, 1992, 1994 refers to this practice as "embedded racism."

[30] See M. Omi, & W. Howard, On the theoretical concept of race. In C. McCarthy, & W. Crichloe (Eds.). *Race identity and representation in education.* (New York: Routledge, 1993)

[31] A. Lareau, & E.M. Horvat, Moments of social inclusion and exclusion: Race, class, and cultural capital in family-school relationships. *Sociology of Education,* 72(1), (1999), 37–53, p. 39.

[32] See Z. Cline & J. Necochea, ¡Basta ya! Latino parents fighting entrenched racism. Bilingual Research Journal, 25 (1&2), (2001), 1–26; Lareau & Horvat; E.M. Olivos *Dialectical tensions, contradictions, and resistance: A study of the relationship between Latino parents and the public school system within a socioeconomic 'structure of dominance.'* (Unpublished doctoral dissertation, San Diego State University/Claremont Graduate University, 2003); A.Y.F. Ramirez, Dismay and disappointment: Parental involvement of Latino immigrant parents. *The Urban Review,* 35(2), (2003), 93–110; S. Shannon, Minority parental involvement: A Mexican mother's experience and a teacher's interpretation. *Education and Urban Society.* 29(1), (1996), 71–84; & S. M. Shannon, & S. Lojero-Latimer, A story of struggle and resistance: Latino parent involvement in the schools. *Journal of Educational Issues of Language Minority Students,* 16, (1996), 301–319 for examples.

[33] Shannon, 1996.

[34] N. Gibbs, Parents behaving badly. Inside the new classroom power struggle: What teachers say about pushy moms and dads who drive them crazy. *Time,* 165 (8), (2005, February 21), 38–49.

[35] M. Fine, [Ap]parent involvement: Reflections on parents, power, and urban public schools. *Teachers College Record.* 94(4), (1993): 682–710, p. 684.

[36] Shannon, 1996.

[37] Mexican American parents frequently use the word "American" synonymously with "Anglo" or "White."

[38] See Cline & Nechochea; R. Galindo, Language wars: The ideological dimensions of the debates on bilingual education. *Bilingual Research Journal,* 21(2 & 3), (1997); M. Mejorado, Parents and community working together: Making a difference. *The Multilingual Educator.* (Special Conference Issue 2005), 20–27; E.M. Olivos, Tensions, contradictions, and resistance: An activist's reflection of the struggles of Latino parents in the public school system. *The High School Journal: Chicana/o Activism in Education: Theories and Pedagogies of Trans/formation,* 87(4), (2004), 25–35; & Ramirez, 2003, for examples of the struggles of Spanish-speaking parents in the school context.

[39] Galindo, p. 121.

[40] Lareau & Horvat, 1999.

[41] G.R. Lopez, *On whose terms? Understanding involvement through the eyes of migrant parents.* Paper presented at the Annual Meeting of the American Educational Research Association (AERA), Seattle, WA. (2001) as cited in Henderson & Mapp, p. 138.

[42] See J. U. Ogbu, & M. A. Matute-Bianchi, Understanding sociocultural factors: Knowledge, identity, and school adjustment. In California Department of Education (Ed.). *Beyond language: Social and cultural factors in schooling language minority students.* (pp. 73–142) (Los Angeles: Evaluation, Dissemination, and Assessment Center, UCLA, 1992).

[43] S. N. Ritblatt, J. R. Beatty, T. A. Cronan, & A. M. Ochoa, Relationships among perceptions of parent involvement, time allocation, and demographic characteristics: Implications for policy formation. *Journal of Community Psychology*. 30(5), (2002), 519–549.

Chapter 5

[1] A. Lareau, & E.M. Horvat, Moments of social inclusion and exclusion: Race, class, and cultural capital in family-school relationships. *Sociology of Education*, 72(1), (1999), 37–53, p. 42.

[2] A. M. Ochoa, Empowering parents to be teachers of their children: The Parent Institute for Quality Education. *Learning communities narratives: Learning from our differences: Color, culture, and class. Part two.* 2 (2). (Cleveland, OH: Learning Communities Network, Inc., 1997), p. 51.

[3] See Z. Cline & J. Necochea, ¡Basta ya! Latino parents fighting entrenched racism. *Bilingual Research Journal*, 25 (1&2), (2001), 1–26; M. Mejorado, Parents and community working together: Making a difference. *The Multilingual Educator.* (Special Conference Issue 2005), 20–27; E.M. Olivos *Dialectical tensions, contradictions, and resistance: A study of the relationship between Latino parents and the public school system within a socioeconomic 'structure of dominance.'* (Unpublished doctoral dissertation, San Diego State University/Claremont Graduate University, 2003); A.Y.F. Ramirez, Dismay and disappointment: Parental involvement of Latino immigrant parents. *The Urban Review*, 35(2), (2003), 93–110; S. Shannon, Minority parental involvement: A Mexican mother's experience and a teacher's interpretation. *Education and Urban Society.* 29(1), (1996), 71–84; & S. M. Shannon, & S. Lojero-Latimer, A story of struggle and resistance: Latino parent involvement in the schools. *Journal of Educational Issues of Language Minority Students*, 16, (1996), 301–319 for examples.

[4] R. Núñez, *Schools, parents, and empowerment: An ethnographic study of Mexican-origin parents participation in their children's schools.* (Unpublished Doctoral Dissertation, San Diego State University/Claremont Graduate School, San Diego, CA/Claremont, CA, 1994).

[5] See J. U. Ogbu, & M. A. Matute-Bianchi, Understanding sociocultural factors: Knowledge, identity, and school adjustment. In California Department of Education (Ed.). *Beyond language: Social and cultural factors in schooling language minority students.* (pp. 73–142) (Los Angeles: Evaluation, Dissemination, and Assessment Center, UCLA, 1992) for theoretical perspectives on caste immigrants, involuntary immigrants, and voluntary immigrants.

[6] Ramirez, p. 99.

[7] Núñez, p. 71.

[8] As cited in J. Cummins, *Negotiating identities: Education for empowerment in a diverse society.* (2nd edition). (Ontario, CA: California Association for Bilingual Education, 2001), p. 8.

[9] A. Darder, *Culture and power in the classroom: A critical foundation for bicultural education.* (Westport, CT: Bergin & Garvey, 1991).

[10] T.K. Arnold, We got trouble right here: Stressed-out students, absentee parents, shrinking budgets—they all take their toll on today's teachers. *San Diego Magazine,* 55 (5), (2003, March), 64–65.; K. Cotton, && K.R. Wikelund, Parent involvement in education. *School Improvement Research Series.* Retrieved October 13, 2002, from http://www.nwrel.org/ scpd/sirs/3/cu6.html; E. Zimmerman, Meet the parents: These days, there's even a school for parents of schoolchildren. The biggest lesson: Just be there for your kids. *San Diego Magazine,* 55 (5), (2003, March), 61–63.

[11] P. Freire, *Teachers as cultural workers: Letters to those who dare to teach.* (Boulder, CO: Westview Press, 1998), p. 39.

[12] P. Freire, *Pedagogy of the oppressed.* (Mayra Bergman Ramos, Trans). (New York: Continuum, 1993).

[13] M. Foucault, *Power/knowledge: Selected interviews & other writings 1972–1977.* (New York: Pantheon Books, 1980).

[14] M. Fine, [Ap]parent involvement: Reflections on parents, power, and urban public schools. *Teachers College Record.* 94(4), (1993): 682–710, p. 682.

[15] A. Lareau, & E.M. Horvat, Moments of social inclusion and exclusion: Race, class, and cultural capital in family-school relationships. *Sociology of Education,* 72(1), (1999), 37–53, p. 42.

[16] P. McLaren, *Life in schools: An introduction to critical pedagogy in the foundation of education.* (2nd edition). White Plains, NY: Longman, 1994), p. 197–198.

[17] See Darder, 1991.

[18] A. Lareau, Social class differences in family-school relationships: The importance of cultural capital. *Sociology of education,* 60 (2), (1987), 73–85, p. 82.

[19] Freire, 1993, p. 133.

[20] J.G. Watts, *Critical pedagogy beyond the classroom: Partnership for systemic change.* (Ontario, CA: California Association for Bilingual Education, 1996), p. 18.

[21] Term used by Shannon, 1996.

[22] M. MacCarthy, Why city schools walkouts matter. *The San Diego Union-Tribune* (2002, December 19).

[23] Cummins, p. 201.

[24] E. Sullivan, *Civil society and school accountability: A human rights approach to parent and community participation in NYC schools.* (New York: Center for Economic and Social Rights, 2003), p. 9.

[25] Cummins, p. 209.

[26] *Ibid.,* p. 205.

Chapter 6

[1] A. Lareau, & E.M. Horvat, Moments of social inclusion and exclusion: Race, class, and cultural capital in family-school relationships. *Sociology of Education,* 72(1), (1999), 37–53, p. 38.

[2] A. Darder, *Culture and power in the classroom: A critical foundation for bicultural education.* (Westport, CT: Bergin & Garvey, 1991), p. 42.

[3] C. H. Persell, *Education and inequality: The roots and results of stratification in America's schools.* (New York: The Free Press, 1977), p. 8.

[4] A. Covarrubias & A. Tijerina-Revilla, Agencies of transformational resistance. *Florida Law Review.* Vol. 55(1) (2003), p. 463.

[5] H. Giroux, *Theory and resistance in education: Towards a pedagogy for the opposition.* (Westport, CT: Bergin & Garvey, 2001), p.107.

[6] J. Cummins, *Negotiating identities: Education for empowerment in a diverse society.* (2nd edition). (Ontario, CA: California Association for Bilingual Education, 2001), pp. 137 & 139.

[7] *Ibid.*, p. 201.

[8] R. Núñez, *Themes on racial factors in education.* (Unpublished doctoral qualifying examination, San Diego State University, 1992), p. 40.

[9] Darder, p. 89.

[10] D. Solórzano, & D. Delgado Bernal, Examining transformational resistance through a critical race and LatCrit theory framework: Chicana and Chicano students in an urban context. *Urban Education,* 36 (3), (2001), 308–342, p. 315.

[11] *Ibid.*, p. 317.

[12] *Ibid.*, p. 317.

[13] *Ibid.*, p. 317.

[14] *Ibid.*, p. 317.

[15] *Ibid.*, p. 317.

[16] For more detail on my work with parents, see E. M. Olivos, *Dialectical tensions, contradictions, and resistance: A study of the relationship between Latino parents and the public school system within a socioeconomic "structure of dominance."* (Unpublished Doctoral Dissertation, San Diego State University/Claremont Graduate School, San Diego, CA/Claremont, CA, 2003); E.M. Olivos, Tensions, contradictions, and resistance: An activist's reflection of the struggles of Latino parents in the public school system. *The High School Journal: Chicana/o Activism in Education: Theories and Pedagogies of Trans/formation,* 87(4), (2004), 25–35.

[17] J. Frederickson, In Darder, A. (Ed.) *Teaching as an act of love: Reflections on Paulo Freire and his contributions to our work.* (pp. 1–18) (Los Angeles, CA: California Association for Bilingual Education, 1998), p. 13.

[18] *Ibid.*, p. 13.

Chapter 7

[1] C.H. Persell, *Education and inequality: The roots and results of stratification in America's schools.* (New York: The Free Press, 1977).

[2] A. Darder, *Culture and power in the classroom: A critical foundation for bicultural education.* (Westport, CT: Bergin & Garvey, 1991), p. 80.

[3] P. McLaren, *Life in schools: An introduction to critical pedagogy in the foundation of education.* (4th edition). (Boston: Allyn & Bacon, 2003), p. 193, (italics in original).

[4] Darder, p. 81.

[5] J. Cummins, *Negotiating identities: Education for empowerment in a diverse society.* (2nd edition). (Ontario, CA: California Association for Bilingual Education, 2001), p. 136.

Chapter 8

[1] E.M. Olivos & A.M. Ochoa, Operationalizing a transformational paradigm of parent involvement in K. Cadiero-Kaplan, A. Ochoa, J. Rodriguez & N. Kuhlman, (Eds.) *The living work of teachers: Ideology and practice with and in community.* (Los Angeles: California Association for Bilingual Education, in press).

[2] These models were originally identified in C. Delgado-Gaitán in *Literacy for empowerment: The role of parents in children's education.* (New York: The Falmer Press, 1990) & S.P. McCaleb in *Building communities of learners.* (New York: St. Martin's Press, 1994).

[3] Delgado-Gaitán, p. 50.

[4] McCaleb, p. 7.

[5] Delgado-Gaitán, p. 51.

[6] Delgado-Gaitán, p. 54.

[7] McCaleb, 1997.

[8] *Ibid.,* p. 26.

[9] A. Darder, *Culture and power in the classroom: A critical foundation for bicultural education.* (Westport, CT: Bergin & Garvey, 1991), p. 94.

[10] Olivos & Ochoa, in press.

[11] This section draws heavily from the work of W. Feinberg & J.F. Soltis, *School and society.* (4th edition) (New York: Teachers College Press, 2004) and their analyses of the relationship between school and society using three lenses: functionalism, conflict theory, and interpretivism.

[12] A. Pearl, & T. Knight, *The democratic classroom.* (Cresskill, New Jersey: Hampton Press, Inc., 1999).

[13] P. Freire, Dialogue is not a Chaste Event. In P. Jurmo (Ed.) *Comments by Paulo Freire on issues in participatory research.* (Amherst, MA: University of Massachusetts, Center for International Education, 1982).

[14] *Ibid.,* p. 69.

[15] A. F. Ada, Creative readings: A relevant methodology for language minority children. In M. Malwe (Ed). *NABE '87. Theory, research and applications: Selected papers.* (Buffalo, NY: State University of New York Press, 1998), pp. 97–111.

[16] H.R. Maturana, & F.J. Varela, *The tree of knowledge.* (Boston: New Science Library, 1987), p. 24.

[17] B. R. Lindsey, N. R. Kikanza, D. Raymond, D. R. Terrell, *Cultural proficiency: A manual for school leaders.* (New York: Corwin Press, Inc., 1999).

Index

A

achievement gap, 15–17, 21, 86
administrators
    and racism, 45, 57
    as agents of change, 104, 120
    as agents of schooling, xi, 3, 5, 51, 55, 90
    as barriers, 5, 95
    blaming parents, 34, 65, 83
    expectations, 52, 102
    hegemonic status of, 30, 37, 68
    relationship with parents, 54, 57, 61

B

Banfield, 47
Beatty, 56
bicultural
    definition of, 14
bicultural parents
    paternalistic treatment of, ix, 55, 58, 68, 102
    perceptions about education, 55–57, 64
Black parents. *See* parents: African-American
blaming the victim, 16, 29, 38, 45, 102
Bowles & Gintis, 34

C

capital
    cultural, 16, 32, 34, 37, 48, 52, 63, 66, 69, 70, 72, 78
    economic, 37, 70
    social, 37, 48, 69, 70, 74
capitalism, x, 16, 27-29, 34-35, 42, 49, 100
    racialized groups and, 28, 34
capitalist system. *See* capitalism
conflict theory, 112, 114
consciousness
    consciousness-raising, 111

    critical, 10, 22, 87
    political, 3, 5, 22, 92, 102, 112
    social, 11
    transformational, 10
Cronan, 56-57
cultural invasion, 72
culture of poverty, 47
Cummins, 49, 75-77, 89, 110

D

Darder, ix, 43, 85, 103, 111
deficit notions. *See* deficit thinking
deficit theories, 45-48
    biological, 46
    cultural, 47
    purpose of, 48
    structural, 46
deficit thinking, xi, 2, 45–49, 59, 67, 101, 109
    in parent involvement, 109
Delgado Bernal, 90–93
democracy
    cultural, 115, 117
    economic, 115
dissonance
    personal, 87
    symbolic, 87
Dunn, 65

E

education
    banking model of, 69
educational reforms
    conservative, 16
    liberal, 16
ELAC. *See* English Learner Advisory Committee
English Learner Advisory Committee, 3, 4, 9, 80, 92
English Learners, 58, 63

Studies in the Postmodern Theory of Education

General Editors
Joe L. Kincheloe & Shirley R. Steinberg

Counterpoints publishes the most compelling and imaginative books being written in education today. Grounded on the theoretical advances in criticalism, feminism, and postmodernism in the last two decades of the twentieth century, Counterpoints engages the meaning of these innovations in various forms of educational expression. Committed to the proposition that theoretical literature should be accessible to a variety of audiences, the series insists that its authors avoid esoteric and jargonistic languages that transform educational scholarship into an elite discourse for the initiated. Scholarly work matters only to the degree it affects consciousness and practice at multiple sites. Counterpoints' editorial policy is based on these principles and the ability of scholars to break new ground, to open new conversations, to go where educators have never gone before.

For additional information about this series or for the submission of manuscripts, please contact:

> Joe L. Kincheloe & Shirley R. Steinberg
> c/o Peter Lang Publishing, Inc.
> 275 Seventh Avenue, 28th floor
> New York, New York 10001

To order other books in this series, please contact our Customer Service Department:

> (800) 770-LANG (within the U.S.)
> (212) 647-7706 (outside the U.S.)
> (212) 647-7707 FAX

Or browse online by series:

> www.peterlangusa.com